Contents

Caring for Older People

Creative approaches to good practice

Terry Smyth, MA, BA, RGN, RMN, DipN, RNT

Head of Community and Educational Studies,
Colchester Institute

Foreword by Professor Heinz Wolff

M
MACMILLAN

This book is dedicated to the memory of two people – to my mother whose positive attitude to life has proved so important to me; and to George Wood, a remarkable teacher and tutor whose tolerance and warmth guaranteed the affection of his students and colleagues alike.

© Terry Smyth 1992

First published 1992 by
THE MACMILLAN PRESS LTD
Houndmills, Basingstoke, Hampshire RG21 2XS
and London
Companies and representatives
throughout the world

ISBN 0–333–57053–7

A catalogue record for this book is available
from the British Library

Filmset by Wearset, Boldon, Tyne and Wear

Printed in Hong Kong

10 9 8 7 6 5 4 3 2 1
01 00 99 98 97 96 95 94 93 92

Foreword

There is some biological evidence that the 'design' life span of wild man was about 50 years; by that time there was a high probability that accident, injury, starvation or disease would have taken its toll. At that age, degenerative disease of all kinds is relatively rare. Since then, improvements in public health, diet, medicine and a less acutely dangerous environment have allowed a substantial fraction of the population in the developed countries to survive into their seventies, eighties and beyond. The big surge in survival is a phenomenon of the last 100 years and is apparently continuing.

There is nothing which has equipped mankind, in evolutionary terms, to deal with the personal problems which are encountered in living to a great age, or for society to assimilate this new section of the population.

It is clear that a proportion of these 'super adults' will be different from the main body of the population because of the physiological and psychological changes which accompany ageing. They may require special provision in terms of personal care, housing, technological aids and psychological support, quite apart from the treatment of specific disease conditions.

This book is addressed to individuals who are training for careers in caring or who are already working in this field, either in paid employment or voluntarily. It is not a 'how to do it' manual in the sense of a book on car maintenance, but seeks to provide a thorough understanding of the state of being elderly and the principles which underlie the way in which problems which do arise can be managed. The term 'managed' should not be taken to imply some heartlessly efficient procedure. This book throughout places great emphasis on the rights of the individual and freedom of choice, wherever and whenever it is possible that these can be exercised.

An important feature of the book is the suggestions for practical work which are given at the end of each section, and the reading lists. The book is therefore not only valuable for the information which is contained between its covers, but it also provides a key to a much wider world which the readers will explore by their own efforts.

I liked it!

Professor Heinz Wolff
Brunel University
Uxbridge

Acknowledgements

I should like to thank those who have helped at various stages in the preparation of this book, in particular Michael Key (Day Services Manager, Derbyshire County Council Social Services Department), Valerie Farebrother (Director, Division of Community and Academic Studies, West Kent College), Emma Lee (Community Support Worker (Mental Health), Westminster Social Services Department), Jan Kermeen (Hospital/Community Liaison, Community Unit, Huntingdon Health Authority) and Stuart Sillars (language consultant to the Macmillan FE care series). I should also like to thank all those students, past and present, who have helped my thoughts on the care of older people to take root.

The author and publishers wish to thank the following for permission to use copyright material:

Age Concern England–extracts from *The Way We Are* by Jeremy Seabrook, 1990–page 5; Age Resource 1990–picture of the Age Exchange Reminiscence and Theatre Group, Blackheath–page 88; Age Resource 1991–Windsurfing with the Seavets–page 6; Woodworking with the Retired and Senior Volunteer Programme, Isle of Wight–page 7; Artwork with the Wandsworth Black Elderly Arts Project–page 7; Gardening with the Retired and Senior Volunteer Programme, Isle of Wight–page 84; Computing with the 'Teaching Older Dogs New Tricks' Programme, Coleraine, Northern Ireland–page 95; Bryan Bennett and Jessica Lowrie–photographs, page 12; John Birdsall and *Care Weekly*–photograph, page 104; *Care Weekly*–photograph, page 19; extract from 'Voyage with My Father', 4 May 1990–page 134; *Care Weekly* and *Southend Evening Echo*–photograph, page 23; Controller of HMSO–extract from the Department of Health and Social Services Inspectorate Report, 1990–page 15; extract from the White Paper, *Caring for People*–page 17; and extracts from NVQ/SVQ statements–pages 150–1; Rob Cousins and *Care Weekly*–photograph, page 27; DePuy Healthcare–illustrations, page 100; Devon and Cornwall Press Agency and *Care Weekly*–photograph, page 138; Essex County Council Social Services Department–extract from its Policy for Residential Care Homes, page 26; Peter Fisher and Jewish Care–photograph, page 84; Adrian Ford and Help the Aged–photograph, page 83; Peter Hayman and Lynda King (Rose Cottage Residential Home, Broughton, Cambs)–photograph, page 41; Help Age International–poem 'Memba Wen', page 91; Angela Martin and *Care Weekly*–cartoon, page 80; Napier House Residential Home, Newcastle-upon-Tyne–photographs, page 24; Nottingham Rehab Ltd–photographs, pages 73, 82, 83, 89, 93, 111, 119; PEPAR Publications–cartoon from 'If You Want Anything Just Ask!' by Gwen Scott, page 113; Honey Salvadori and Age Concern–photographs, page 106; Andrew Wiard and *Care Weekly*–photograph, page 7; Winslow Press and Help the Aged–extract from 'Take Care of Yourself' by Fiona von Zwanenberg, 1988, pages 106–7.

Every effort has been made to trace all copyright holders, but if any have been inadvertently overlooked the publishers will be pleased to make the necessary arrangement at the first opportunity.

1 About this book

An increasing number of older people are needing care, whether at home, in day-care units or in residential care. This book provides essential knowledge and skills that you need in order to care for older clients in an effective and creative way.

Who is this book for?

The contents of the book should be of equal value whether you are someone working in the care sector or a college student following a care course.

- If you are already employed as a full- or part-time care worker, you will find that the book builds on your existing skills and knowledge, and helps you to prepare for assessment for National Vocational Qualifications (NVQs) and Scottish Vocational Qualifications (SVQs), up to and including level 3.

- As a full- or part-time college student – taking, for example, BTEC or City & Guilds qualifications in care – you will find that the book covers most of what you need to know about care of the older person. All such courses now include extensive work experiences that give you the opportunity to develop practical skills and understanding. Many work-based activities have been included to help you achieve this.

- Students following courses leading to professional qualifications in social work will find the book a useful introduction to the topic.

The aims of the book

The purpose of this book is to improve the quality of care for older people by inviting you to discover just how exciting, creative and rewarding this field of work can be. Sadly, many people are content with the impression that caring for older people is strenuous, distressing and depressing. It certainly *can* be all of these things, but it is also much more.

Being able to offer help and care to older clients is an opportunity to help improve other people's lives. Although now receiving care, all your clients have had rich and varied lives – and you can learn a great deal from their experiences. To make a good job of this you need the ability to think clearly and objectively about other people's problems, and commitment to discover your own attitudes and values.

This book aims to show you how this can be achieved in a stimulating and comprehensive way. I have paid particular attention to the development of positive attitudes and the skills of problem-solving. These are more enduring than knowledge on its own, which tends quickly to become out of date. I have also tried to show how important it is to apply the principles of anti-discrimination and anti-racism. These have been integrated throughout. Everyone concerned with care must be able to look on all clients and colleagues as individuals and allow them the chance to express that individuality freely and without being limited by others' prejudice.

The structure of the book

The book is divided into short sections grouped together to form a logical sequence.

- The 'Background' sections (Chapter 2) put care of the older client into its wider social context.
- 'Organising care' (Chapter 3) looks at what caring is and where it takes place; the chapter then describes in detail the ways in which care can be planned.
- 'Implementing care' (Chapter 4) contains a wide range of approaches to practical care, covering communication, activities and learning, relationships, physical care, mental health care, and how to deal with loss and bereavement.
- The final chapter discusses ways of measuring the quality of care.

The book is organised in this way to convey the idea that, whatever the care setting, the older client is an individual like anyone else with a mixture of psychological, social, physical and spiritual needs. This is why care planning is dealt with first; deciding what to do – *implementation* – can come only after you have discovered the needs of the individual.

How to use the book

You can use this book independently or with a supervisor. Most sections include activities, some of which you will first need to discuss and agree with your workplace supervisor; others can be done without help. Even when you work alone, always try to discuss your work with a colleague or tutor. You will get much more out of the book if you do.

Most activities encourage you to reflect on your experience – to analyse what occurred and to try to make sense of it. You should take time to develop these skills – they are needed both for employment and for any further study you may do. In caring, it is not enough simply to follow instructions – you must understand what the client feels and search for creative ways to meet his or her needs.

One way of helping to make the best possible use of this book and your experiences is to develop the habit of keeping a written record of your learning. This may be required in some of the activities, or by your supervisor or tutor. Always try to keep a log or diary of your work experience – to record what you felt at the time and how, later, you were able to interpret the experience.

Topics have been arranged in short sections so that you can organise your learning effectively. Together with your supervisor or tutor, you should decide which sections suit your needs at any particular time. You can then arrange a programme of learning which will ensure that you get the most from your work experiences.

Terms used

What should we call the older person who finds himself or herself in need of care? At the moment, *client* is most common in the social-care field, *patient* in health care. Because most older people in care are not in a health setting, I use the term *client* or *older person*.

Why 'older', and not 'elderly', person? It's a matter of encouraging a change in thinking in order to break patterns in attitudes. Since there is no agreed definition of old age, it seems inappropriate to speak of the elderly as if they were a separate species with characteristics different from others. To me, 'older person' seems to suggest fewer rigid divisions. Nevertheless, whenever the term 'client' or 'older person' is used in the book, I hope you will be able to bring the words to life by trying to picture an actual person.

I have chosen to use the term *care workers* to mean people who are either employed in caring or who are being educated and trained in caring skills.

What are NVQs and SVQs?

As part of the need for a better-trained workforce, NVQs and SVQs are now available for every major occupation. The Care Sector Consortium is the body responsible for ensuring that qualifications in care are relevant and realistic. All NVQs/SVQs are based on the skills needed in real work situations. In time, all existing care qualifications will conform to the requirements of NVQ/SVQ.

> National Vocational Qualifications are about being able to do a job well. NVQs are based on standards developed by industry and commerce. This makes them relevant to work and valued by employers.
>
> Each NVQ is made up of a number of separate units. The units set out exactly what the candidate must be able to do and to what standard. Units are like mini-qualifications: they act as targets for training and credits in certification.
>
> (From *Brief Guide: NVQ* published by the National Council for Vocational Qualifications)

To obtain an NVQ/SVQ, you have to register as a candidate through an approved assessment centre. If you are working in care at the moment, your employer should be able to tell you more; your place of work may itself be an assessment centre.

Assessment is carried out by work-based assessors. They will decide whether or not you are competent by observing your performance while you are working – the most valid type of assessment.

If you are following a course in college, your tutors will be able to advise you on NVQs/SVQs. Many college courses are firmly based on relevant work skills already. Some incorporate NVQs/SVQs; others will prepare you for taking them later, when you are in employment.

General NVQs (GNVQs) are being introduced to allow full-time school and college students to gain vocational qualifications. They are occupationally related but broad enough to allow you to keep your options open.

To find out more about available NVQs/SVQs, ask for further information from your employer, tutor, local further education college or careers service.

2 Background

2.1 Growing older

Who are older people?

'Older people' are simply you and me at a particular point in our lives. Although ageing creates new needs, the essence of the individual remains very much the same: we do not stop being one person, and suddenly become someone else. As a care worker, you need to see the older person as he or she really is and not as just another representative of an age group.

What is old age?

Ageing proceeds at different rates in different people. Simply knowing someone's age is unlikely to tell us a great deal about their individual characteristics or needs.

'Old age' is defined in different ways for different purposes. Most of us are familiar with using retirement as the point beyond which we regard someone as being old. But with early retirements being commonplace in industry and commerce, this may become less and less reliable.

Social and health services often choose an age after which social and treatment needs are dealt with by different groups of specialists. Hence, we have geriatricians (medical consultants who deal exclusively with older clients), and specialist nurses and social workers in the care of older people. With more people now living to a healthy old age, these age boundaries are progressively being pushed back. For example, some specialist services for older clients only deal with people over the age of 70 rather than 65. And under the government's new contracts for general practitioners in Britain, it is patients over 75 who have to be offered a home visit each year to assess physical, social and mental well-being.

Being older: what people say

Being old can come as a surprise:

> 'I don't feel I'm old. When I was younger I always thought I would know when I was old . . . but it doesn't feel how I expected it to at all. I have to remind myself how old I am!'

> 'It's other people's reactions, really. Not something inside. They let you know you're getting on. I wish I could tell them how I feel inside.'

> 'I can't do what I used to. But it only dawned on me slowly. You get out of breath quicker and there are a lot more aches and pains than there used to be.'

ACTIVITY

Think about the quotations on this page.

- How do they make you feel?
- What do you think you will say when you are 80 years of age?

Discuss your views with colleagues and your supervisor.

ACTIVITY

When next you meet older acquaintances of yours, try to imagine them as they used to be: at middle age, or in their early twenties, or as teenagers. You may find this difficult at first, but persist with it. Use old photographs as well.

Ask them about their pasts and try to build up a picture of how they see themselves. Be very tactful and sensitive at all times, however, to avoid any sense of intrusion.

Reading on . . .

★ *The Way We Are*, by Jeremy Seabrook, published by Age Concern in 1980, is a series of personal accounts by older people from a wide range of backgrounds.

★ *Famous Ways to Grow Old*, by Phillip Bristow, is a collection of letters from a large number of distinguished men and women who were asked to offer advice on growing old. Contributors include Barbara Cartland, Charlton Heston and Mother Teresa. It was published by Age Concern in 1989.

J.B. Priestley's reply to the question of what it was like to be old combines wisdom and gentle humour:

'It was as though walking down Shaftesbury Avenue as a fairly young man, I was suddenly kidnapped, rushed into a theatre and made to don the grey hair, the wrinkles and other attributes of age, then wheeled on-stage. Behind the appearance of age I am the same person, with the same thoughts, as when I was younger.'

The past is often reconsidered in old age and this reappraisal may be linked to beliefs that are held about life in general:

'I can only think that God has turned away from man because of the way we have treated each other. . . . Now I'm old I've a lot of leisure to think about it like I never did when I was younger. I had my work on the railway, the family. . . . I want to believe and I can't.'

(Seabrook 1980, p. 94)

'The life I've led, my dear, you wouldn't believe it . . . lovers, I've broken hearts as readily as other people break promises. . . . One very highly placed official was going to shoot his brains out if I wouldn't sleep with him. . . . The only thing I regret now is that I didn't use my physical advantages for financial security.'

(Seabrook 1980, p. 97)

'Being poor, what is it? I've never been anything else, so I couldn't really tell you. I can tell you where every penny of my money goes . . . I like going to the local shops. I like to see what I can get a bit cheaper. I like to talk to people but there's a lot of them haven't got the time of day for you if you're a bit older. They're afraid you might ask them for something. They more or less ignore you, pass you by, they think you can't be very interesting if you're old. Being old today, well if poverty isn't a crime, old age is.'

(Seabrook 1980, pp. 107, 109)

'I wouldn't change my life. Even if I had to live it all over again, I wouldn't want it any different. I feel I've learned from my experience, I've learned what the good things are in life. Not material things. I don't covet anything. . . . When I think of it, I think we've lost more than we've gained. All the people in this town used to leave their doors open all day, the gasman would come, empty the meters, leave the rebate on the kitchen table, you knew it was safe.'

(Seabrook 1980, pp. 103–4)

Having a different ethnic background introduces new insights:

'In England, when you reach 60 or 65 years old, you become a social problem. No one cares about you . . . if you are ill, that makes it worse. In the West Indies you don't finish at 60 or 65 – you are respected. The older you are, the more respected you are.'

(Norman 1985, p. 2)

It is vital for care workers to know something of how clients view their own old age, what their beliefs are and how they see their past, present and future. These are not always easy topics to talk about. Whether or not clients will want to talk about such things depends on your relationship with them. Do they trust you enough to disclose beliefs of this kind? These topics will be taken up in more detail in later sections.

2.2 Images and impressions of old age

Our attitudes to old age and older people are shaped by many factors – for example, our upbringing, education, experiences, and the media. Being an effective care worker means being aware of these influences, and the ways in which they may help or hinder the quality of care offered to clients. It is not just the attitudes of staff that matter. Older people themselves have attitudes to old age – and, as with care workers and *their* attitudes, some of these will be helpful, others not.

Myths about old age

Old age suffers from misunderstanding probably more than any other stage of life. There are many myths and mostly they are unattractive. Amongst the various popular misconceptions about old age are the following:

- All older people are much the same.
- Older people cannot learn new things, are set in their ways and cannot change.
- Most older people have no interest in sexual behaviour.
- All older people will eventually suffer from memory loss and dementia.
- Most older people are ill.
- Most older people need residential care.
- Afro-Caribbean and Asian older people always live with their families and don't need help from the caring services.
- Older people are a drain on society and are unable to offer anything useful.
- Older people should be careful and not take risks.
- Most older people like to be looked after and spoiled.

How is it that so many incorrect views are held about older people in general and then thoughtlessly applied to individuals? *Stereotyping* is the term used to describe this process: stereotypes are incorrect, oversimplified beliefs about a group or category of people, in this case older people. By using stereotypes, we avoid the harder work of looking at individuals as they really are. Here are some examples of how stereotypes might affect care practice:

Stereotype: *older people cannot learn new things.*

> Miss Jones is very severely disabled with arthritis and has been in residential care for the past nine months. She retired 12 years ago from a post as an administrator. Although she found the job challenging, she still feels that she has unrealised potential. She is invited to participate in various activities in the home (such as handicrafts, singing and quizzes), but does so reluctantly. Staff tend to regard her as an uncooperative resident who sees herself as superior to the others. Her needs are not being met and no one has discussed with her the possibilities of taking further study, perhaps with the Open University.

Stereotypes: *most older people have no interest in sexual behaviour; sexual behaviour in old age is inappropriate, silly or sinful.*

> Mr Lee, a widower, is living at home with support both from relatives and professional care workers. He cannot get around easily because of a stroke three years ago and so most of his time is spent in his sheltered flat. While tidying up during a recent visit, the care worker uncovered a number of books containing sexually explicit photographs. Mr Lee said that his grandson must have left them behind. In the flurry of embarrassed activity that followed, the care worker put them away in a cupboard out of Mr Lee's reach.

ACTIVITY

1 Select three instances where older people are portrayed in the mass media – in newspapers, on radio or television. Can you detect any myths about old age? You might like to focus especially on:

- television series like EastEnders, Coronation Street, Golden Girls or The Archers;
- magazines of different types – Sunday supplements, magazines targeted specifically at women, or gardening magazines, for example;
- advertisements in newspapers and magazines, and on television;
- films and television plays;
- jokes and comedy programmes on television.

2 Can you find any examples of efforts to get away from the stereotype?

Stereotypes have no place in the caring services. But the problem does not go away easily – it has to be worked at. Section 4.9 covers this topic in more depth.

Of course, challenging stereotypes about old age in this way does not make everything all right overnight. Neither does it make old age the best time of your life. It would be incorrect to suggest that increasing age doesn't mean greater likelihood of illness and disability: it does. But this does not mean that old age is a stage of life to be feared. Many older people are healthy until the very end of their lives. And, for many people, childhood and adolescence, or adulthood, haven't been without their problems either.

ACTIVITY

In traditional societies older people are encouraged to pass on moral values to the younger generations. Because they are less involved with everyday demands – work, family and so on – they can concentrate on the basic aspects of their culture. Contrast this with Western societies in which older people struggle to find a useful role. Freedom from the daily grind can be of great benefit to society. Older people can be more forceful and independent because they have to worry less about the immediate reactions of others. For example, older lawyers were more active than their younger counterparts in bringing down President Richard Nixon over the Watergate affair.

1 Can you recognise from your own experience ways in which older people protect and pass on our basic moral and cultural values? Not everyone will agree on what these values are, but they could include the following:

- believing in the rights of the individual;
- the need for a system of justice in society;
- the importance of the family.

2 Discuss with colleagues and your supervisor how you could use these ideas to improve the care of clients. For example, how often do you encourage clients to talk about their beliefs and values? How could you do this?

2.3 An ageing population

Social and medical advances have resulted in many more people living to an old age. This isn't to say that we can now make it to 130 years – we can't. But it does mean that we can all reasonably expect to live to a ripe, and usually healthy, old age. The average child born in Britain today will live some 25 years longer than was the case in 1900 – a dramatic increase.

Another important change since 1900 is that fewer babies are being born in Western industrial societies. These two trends have led to a different population structure, with fewer younger people and more older people. As a result, in Britain there are now roughly as many over-60s as there are under-16s.

Statistics of this kind help us to understand some of the major changes taking place in society, such as the need to develop housing, health-care and social-care services and pension arrangements that are appropriate to an ageing population. The picture is complex, however, as the following statistics show.

> Those over retirement age in Britain
> (65 for men, 60 for women):
>
> 1991 – 10 million
> 2021 – 12 million
> 2051 – 12 million

According to these statistics, there will be a levelling off in the numbers of older people; but these figures hide some important facts. If the percentage of the very old is looked at as well, the position is different:

> Percentage over 85 years:
>
> 1991 –   8%
> 2021 – 10%
> 2051 – 15%

The problem for society then is going to be how to meet the needs of people in their eighties and nineties who are likely to need increasing levels of support.

> Living alone:
>
> 66% of couples over 65 live alone
> 50% of women over 75 live on their own

Although this may seem a recipe for loneliness and perhaps depression, this is not necessarily the case. Older people often have a great deal of contact with grandchildren. Be careful, therefore, not to confuse living alone with being cut off and lonely. 'Intimacy at a distance' is an expression that has been used to describe a situation where there is regular contact with relatives and friends despite living some distance apart. It is worth remembering too that many people choose to live alone well before retirement.

Sexuality and gender

Men and women currently have very different experiences during the later stages of their lives. Because women generally outlive men, it is not surprising that there are more women living on their own, or that there are more women in need of help from the caring services. Nevertheless, as we have seen in an earlier section, stereotypes of old age are important factors in our approach to care. Older women have to deal with two kinds of stereotype: those related to being older and those related to being a woman.

One common stereotype is that women are able instinctively to care for others, and therefore for themselves as well. This encourages inadequate provision by the caring services. Some older women, because of this insidious sexism, may also fall into the trap of seeing themselves as needing to be all-capable. Should a woman need residential care, her own care may be influenced by the fact that care workers expect her to have been an expert in looking after others.

Gay and lesbian clients are also faced with the problem of being treated as stereotypes. Some care workers may find homosexuality in clients very disturbing and may resort to using social stereotypes to deal with it. Attitudes are changing slowly, however, and the care worker can contribute to this by always trying to respond to the individual, not the stereotype.

Race

It is difficult to obtain accurate information about numbers of older people from different ethnic origins. The term 'ethnic minority' is often used but is difficult to define in such a way that makes comparison between the numbers straightforward. Nevertheless, many official statistics continue to use it.

Ethnic minorities (1981 Census)
Total: 2.2 million (4.2% of total population of Great Britain)
The numbers of pensionable age are:

Ireland –	132 000
Old Commonwealth –	21 000
India –	44 000
Caribbean –	16 000
Pakistan –	4 800
Far East –	3 900
Bangladesh –	3 800
Mediterranean –	3 700

Like women, and like minority groups in society such as the physically or mentally handicapped, people from different ethnic origins are inclined to be stereotyped in unhelpful ways. Take, for example, the belief that all older Afro-Caribbean and Asian people live as part of an extended family network and so need fewer social services. In Britain it probably *is* true that more families from other ethnic origins place a high priority on caring for their older relatives than do white English families. But it doesn't *always* happen that way. The inability to provide this family care may result in a great deal of shame and stigma for both the family and older relative.

Every industrialised country is having to come to terms with an increasing proportion of older people. We should realise that this creates great opportunities as well as great demands on the social and health services. Too many people are inclined to think of the problems and to neglect the advantages of this changing social picture. In the course of your work, and outside it, *you* can play an important role in trying to break down negative attitudes towards older people.

ACTIVITY

1 Try to find some of the relevant population statistics for your area. Many authorities produce easy-to-read statistical summaries. They need to gather a great deal of local information for their own planning purposes and are usually ready to pass this on. Useful local sources are:

- the local authority (start with the town hall if you aren't sure of the exact department);
- social services department;
- district health authority;
- county council.

2 Use these statistics to try to understand better the clients in your care setting. Try to answer the following questions.

- What is the number (and the percentage) of retired people in your area?
- What is the percentage of over-85s?
- Are there any statistics available showing how many older people are from ethnic minority groups?
- How many of your clients moved to the area after they retired?

3 Discuss with colleagues and your supervisor the implications of these statistics for your care setting – for example, the likely changes in demand over the next ten years and how the service will need to respond.

2.4 A positive view of ageing

Throughout this book, the positive aspects of ageing are emphasised. But ageing doesn't become positive just by asserting that it should be. In this section, some evidence is provided for why we should adopt a more optimistic view of old age and what it can offer.

Erik Erikson – making sense of life

In *Childhood and Society*, Erik Erikson, a famous American psychotherapist, described eight stages of life. His work is important because he tried to explain how humans develop over their whole lifespan, in contrast to many others who have written about human development up to adulthood, as if development practically stopped in mid-life and old age hardly existed.

Erikson says that in the final stages of life we hope to reach a state that he called 'ego integrity'. In simple language, this means experiencing a sense of meaning and order, both for ourselves and in the way we see the world around us; to be able to feel ourselves as unique and as having followed a path through life that was, and is, ours alone. We achieve this sense of completeness through thinking about our successes and failures, trying to give them meaning and putting them into context.

Erikson wrote:

> Each individual, to become a mature adult, must develop to a sufficient degree all of the ego qualities, so that a wise Indian, a true gentleman, and a mature peasant share and recognise in one another the final stage of integrity.
>
> (Erikson 1963)

These ideas are not easy but think about them and try to keep them in mind when caring for your older clients. Erikson reminds us that every individual is of equal worth and that this belief must underpin all our actions in caring for clients.

ACTIVITY

1 Perhaps putting our successes and failures into context is something we should be doing throughout our lives. If we do this as we go along, we will not have such a major task when we reach our final years. Ask yourself the following questions.

- How often do I think back over my life and try to make sense of it as a whole?
- Can I see a pattern in my life? If so, is it one that I feel satisfied with? If not, what kind of pattern would I like to see?

- Are there periods in my life which would be difficult to fit into a pattern that I could understand?
- Can I do things in the future that would help me to make more sense of the past?

2 Although this is a very personal exercise, it would be helpful to share your responses with your supervisor.

Gains – new roles in life

When describing old age, many people talk only of losses – loss of job, loss of status, loss of money, for example – which can bring about a sense of depression and hopelessness. But for many older people there are opportunities to develop new roles. Various ideas will emerge in later sections of this book. For the moment, let's look at the role of grandparent.

Grandparenting

Contacts between grandparents and their grandchildren are often quite frequent despite the fact that it is unusual for them all to live in the same house. For some people, the role of grandparent begins at quite an early age (say, in their forties) but can extend well into advanced old age (and into 'great-grandparenting'). Not only can grandparenting be satisfying in itself but it gives people the chance to develop new roles and behaviours, to continue to learn and to challenge preconceived ideas. To summarise – grandparenting can help older people to feel that they are:

- contributors to their family's future;
- providing things that they couldn't give to their own children;
- helping their grandchildren to achieve more than earlier generations;
- loved and respected by their grandchildren

There are many different ways of being a grandparent:

- *Formal* The traditional role: grandparents provide treats, buy presents, often baby-sit.
- *Fun-seeker* A very informal style. This is a free role with little attempt to control the grandchildren. Grandparents and grandchildren join in leisure and play activities.

- *Surrogate-parent* Taking the place of the parents: grandparents here are often the main caretakers of the grandchildren. This usually occurs when both parents go out to work.
- *The source of family wisdom* Grandparents have special knowledge. Particular skills and expertise may be needed indefinitely; for example, families may draw on the extensive experience of grandparents when it comes to making critical business decisions. Alternatively, a retired schoolteacher may be able to help a grandchild with academic work.
- *Distant figure* Grandparents live some way away from children and grandchildren. Visits may be infrequent, perhaps only during holidays. The grandparents are seen as kindly yet remote. Family mobility and the practice of retiring to the coast are some of the reasons for this role developing.

ACTIVITY

In discussion with your colleagues and supervisor, answer the following questions.

- Do you provide your clients with what they need in order to experiment with different roles? For example, are there facilities – such as children's games, tapes, videos – to allow clients to play the role of 'fun-seeker'

with their grandchildren? Or do they prefer the more traditional role?

- Can you think of creative ways in which you could encourage your clients to develop new roles? What about clients who have no family, or who are gay or lesbian? In what ways might you help them to extend their range of roles?

3 Organising care

3.1 The nature of caring: *What is caring?*

The word 'care' is used a good deal in our everyday lives. We care:

- about our appearance;
- for our children or parents;
- about the environment;
- for the clients.

So what does 'caring' mean? Dictionary definitions include 'to have regard or consideration for' and 'to provide help or comfort'. By carrying out the exercises on this page, you will gain an idea of your own attitudes to caring. It is important to realise that you, like every other care worker, will have your own philosophy of care – your own idea of what it means.

ACTIVITY

1 With a colleague, think about the word 'care' in connection with the older person. List all the ideas that spring to mind. Try it this way:

'*Care is* ....
....,
....'
and so on.

2 When you have finished, discuss the list with your colleagues and supervisor. Which ideas are valuable and which unclear? How can you explain differences between your own views and those of your colleagues?

3 If you speak a language other than English, try doing the exercise in this language. Do you notice any differences? Does it make the same sense?

In one research study a group of Canadian nurses were asked to say what caring meant to them. Their responses included the following.

- *Being there* – a physical and emotional presence.
- *Respect* – recognising the client's individuality.
- *Feeling with and for* – being able to see things from the client's point of view.
- *Closeness* – valuing the relationship.
- *Touching and holding* – physical contact for comfort.
- *Picking up cues* – being aware of subtle communications.
- *Being firm* – saying 'no' when necessary.
- *Knowing them well* – keeping in touch with clients.
- *Teaching* – giving information and skills to increase independence.

ACTIVITY

Discuss this list with colleagues. Which items are closest to your own ideas of caring? Would you have added any others?

(The list is based on research results described in Forrest 1989.)

Although jobs in the caring occupations differ a good deal, all care workers are expected to base their actions on common principles designed to promote good practice. The Care Sector Consortium – a body made up of representatives from all parts of the caring services – has set out the following principles of good practice to guide the actions of care workers:

- the rights of all individuals within society should be promoted and supported so that equality and quality of life is available to each individual within the service ...
- each individual should be treated as a whole person with a variety of needs
- anti-discriminatory practice should be developed and promoted so that each individual is guaranteed the same quality of service
- the confidentiality of information and its sources should be respected and disclosed only to those who necessarily require it and after agreement with the individual concerned
- all involved in the delivery of care are essential and integral to the care team (consistent with client choice) and therefore clients and their partners, relatives, friends and community should be involved at all stages
- the health and safety of workers, clients, their partners, relatives and friends is of paramount importance ...
- every individual should be encouraged to be as independent as possible and to exercise informed choice ...
- individual choice, wishes and preferences should be confirmed with the individual and respected in actions taken
- communication (verbal and/or non-verbal) should be that most appropriate to the individual

(Care Sector Consortium 1991, p. vii)

If treated seriously, these principles could be revolutionary. Historically, much care for older people has been too influenced by what the caring services thought best. Consider this principle: *Every individual should be encouraged to be as independent as possible and to exercise informed choice.* Try applying it to your own experience. Care workers sometimes limit their expectations of clients in ways that can restrict their independence – almost a case of 'caring' too much.

Formal and informal carers

Most care for older people is provided by informal carers – relatives, friends and neighbours. In 1991, the Family Policy Studies Centre estimated that there were over 4.5 million informal carers in Great Britain looking after older people – usually a husband, wife or parent. A significant but smaller role is played by those who have committed themselves to working with this client group: the formal care workers.

Fortunately for the future of the caring services, most informal carers are happy to carry on with this role. But the costs are very high. A study undertaken by the Welsh National School of Medicine in 1986 showed that caring carried with it three main costs: financial loss; lost leisure; stress. Of these carers, 25 per cent said that their own health had worsened and 20 per cent reported high stress levels. Depression and anxiety were often present, especially amongst daughters in this role.

The boundaries between formal and informal carers are becoming increasingly blurred. There are a number of schemes in operation which provide payment for care by friends and neighbours. The statutory services are unlikely ever to be able to meet all the care needs of the older person. In view of the strains of informal caring, formal care workers have a vital role to play in supporting the client's relatives and friends in their tasks. This issue is dealt with more fully in section 3.13.

3.2 The nature of caring: *Beliefs a*

What we believe affects how we act. This section deals with the different beliefs and values – the different philosophies – that care workers hold about their clients and their jobs in general. It develops the ideas presented in section 3.1.

In 1990 the Social Services Inspectorate published a report about the care of older people in residential homes. It proposed six important values that ought to form the basis of good-quality care for the older person. Although concerned with residential care, the values seem to apply to good care in general. They are:

- *Choice* – 'the opportunity to select independently from a range of options'.
- *Rights* – 'the maintenance of all entitlements associated with citizenship'.
- *Fulfilment* – 'the realisation of personal aspirations and abilities in all aspects of daily life'.
- *Independence* – 'opportunities to think and act without reference to another person including a willingness to incur a degree of calculated risk'.
- *Privacy* – 'the right to be alone or undisturbed and free from intrusion, or public attention in relation to individuals and their affairs'.
- *Dignity* – 'a recognition of the intrinsic value of people regardless of circumstances by respecting their uniqueness and their personal needs'.

(Department of Health Social Services Inspectorate 1990)

As in many official documents, the language used is rather formal. Most care workers would probably choose to express their beliefs differently, perhaps more directly and personally. What really matters is not the language used but the ideas and behaviour that result from particular beliefs.

In the previous section we began to look at the question of 'independence'. If I believe in the independence of clients, then I have to search for ways in which they can make decisions that I, as the care worker, may not know about and should not wish to know about. This could apply to many situations and will depend on a number of factors, such as the physical and mental health of the client concerned. But what this list of values can do is to make us think about what we do every day, and challenge us to look for new ways. Values are ideals; like all ideals, they can never be realised in full. However, they can inspire us to achieve higher standards.

ACTIVITY

1 Use the ideas in this section to examine the philosophy of care used in your own care setting. This can be done by completing the table. In the *Rating* column write 'poor', 'satisfactory' or 'good'; in the *Comments* column write a few words to support your judgement.

2 Discuss this activity with colleagues and, as far as possible, try to agree on each rating. Where there is a written philosophy of care, does it cover these values? Is there any difference between the philosophy as it is written and the way it is expressed in practice?

Value	Rating	Comments
Choice	....	....
Rights	....	....
Fulfilment	....	....
Independence	....	....
Privacy	....	....
Dignity	....	....

ACTIVITY

1 Choose one of the values in the list given on the previous page. Find three ways to put it into practice in your care setting. Repeat this for each of the other values. Then answer these questions.

- Do you really believe in each of these values?
- Which values do you think might be the hardest to put into practice?

- Do you think your colleagues share your values? How do you know?

2 Discuss your answers with colleagues and your supervisor. Are there ways care could be changed in your setting to reflect these values more strongly? How would your behaviour have to change to help to achieve this?

One way of helping to ensure that care workers *do* manage this is to build these principles into a philosophy of care for the particular work setting, whether this is a care home, a day unit or domiciliary service. An example is given below.

A philosophy of care

These extracts are taken from the philosophy document used by a small private residential home.

At the outset, we feel it important to state our belief that the quality of care offered to the residents should be of the same standard that we would expect for ourselves or our relatives. The ways in which this care is implemented must reflect the wishes of each resident and the needs of the group as a whole. By adopting this approach, we hope that our residents, together with care workers, are able to grow and develop personally and create for themselves a fulfilling and realistic lifestyle.

By drawing upon the extensive local knowledge and personal contacts of the proprietors and other care staff, an individual programme of care is negotiated with each resident. This helps to establish a sense of purpose, essential to the development of self-confidence and self-esteem. Regular progress reviews are in operation which involve the resident, care staff and professional staff as appropriate.

Personal care is available to assist each resident to carry out the normal activities of daily living, which include:

- dressing and undressing;
- personal cleanliness and general physical care;
- a balanced diet;
- effective communication;
- interests and leisure activities;
- meeting learning needs;
- social and group activities;
- meeting spiritual needs.

Medications are administered as necessary in those instances where self-medication is not considered appropriate. Wherever possible, residents are encouraged to maintain their contacts with relatives and friends, and to form new relationships.

We seek the views of residents, individually and as a group, on the everyday running of the home, so that the more routine aspects of care match the needs of the residents as closely as possible . . . we see ourselves as an integral part of the expanding network of community-care facilities in the area. We are committed to working with social and health service staff in order to secure for each resident the best possible care available.

No philosophy of care is perfect. What matters is how far it: conforms to the expectations of clients; rests firmly on the commitment of the staff; reflects current beliefs about standards of care.

ACTIVITY

How far do you think this philosophy matches the values outlined by the Social Services Inspectorate? In discussion with colleagues and your supervisor, try to analyse each part of the philosophy in terms of the six values.

Reading on . . .

★ The Department of Health Social Services Inspectorate produced the guide mentioned in this section – *Caring for Quality: guidance on standards for residential homes for elderly people* (HMSO, 1990).

3.3 Settings for care

The care of the older client takes place in many settings. Wherever possible, the aim should be for this care to take place without the client having to leave his or her own home on a permanent basis.

In 1989 the White Paper, *Caring for People*, put it this way:

> Community care means providing the right level of intervention and support to enable people to achieve maximum independence and control over their own lives. For this aim to become a reality, the development of a wide range of services provided in a variety of settings is essential. These services form part of a spectrum of care, ranging from domiciliary support provided to people in their own homes, strengthened by the availability of respite care and day care for those with more intensive care needs, through sheltered housing, group homes and hostels where increasing levels of care are available, to residential care and nursing homes and long-stay hospital care for those for whom other forms of care are no longer enough.
>
> (HMSO 1989, p. 9, para. 2.2)

Following on from this, the National Health Service and Community Care Act 1990 requires 'packages of care' to be designed for individual clients on the basis of a proper assessment of their needs. In this way, some older people who would otherwise have found their way into residential care may be able to be supported in their own homes for longer. The aim is to provide more flexible and more individual services.

The care of the client will be very much in the hands of two key people: the *care manager* and the *key worker*. The care manager will have overall responsibility for both the costs and the effectiveness of the package of care provided. On a day-to-day basis, however, it is the key worker who will deal most directly with the client. The relationship between these two people is crucial. In the past, a great deal of criticism has been levelled at the way care has been organised in the community. It is all too easy for the lines of communication between workers to break down leading to confusion and neglect of the client. Older people, and in particular those for whom English is not their first language, are especially vulnerable to muddles in communication. Care workers must do all they can to ensure that such mistakes don't happen.

This change in the law will mean a wider range of roles for the care worker – for example, some may be expected to care for clients both in their own homes and in day centres.

Types of care facility

Broadly speaking, specialist facilities are of three main types:

- domiciliary care;
- day care;
- residential care.

Domiciliary care

Here services are taken to the client's home. Examples are the home care service (home helps, care attendants, home care assistants), meals-on-wheels and community occupational therapy. Most of these services are provided by local authority social services departments, often in conjunction with a range of voluntary organisations. The private sector may well increase its involvement in the future.

Day care

Again this may be provided by the public, voluntary or private sectors. 'Nine-to-five' care is offered in day centres in the community, usually from one to five days a week (Monday to Friday), according to need and resources.

Residential care

This may be provided in the public sector by social services departments (funded through central and local taxation), by voluntary organisations (funded by specific fund-raising, legacies and grants from local authorities or commerce) and the private sector (funded by income from the clients themselves). The length of stay can vary from a few days to many years. Residential establishments are categorised legally into 'care' or 'nursing' homes, although many offer both kinds of care to older people. A different authority is responsible for the monitoring of standards in each – local authority social services departments in the case of care homes, and district health authorities in the case of nursing homes.

ACTIVITY

Discuss the following questions with your colleagues and supervisor.

- Why is care being provided in these different ways?
- Think about the clients you care for. Do you feel that they are receiving care in the most appropriate setting, or combinations of settings?
- What types of care would you like to see that are not available at present?

Packages of care

Mr Goldstein

Mr Goldstein is a 73-year-old bachelor. He has lived in the same comfortable flat for the past twenty years. However, in recent months his memory has begun to fail and he often forgets to get himself proper meals or to wash. He has been assessed by the home care organiser (care manager) who has offered domiciliary help three days per week and attendance at a local day centre twice a week. With this support, and some help from a niece and a neighbour, he should be able to remain in his own home.

A care plan is designed in conjunction with the key worker – Mr Goldstein's home care assistant – who will provide direct care in his home and also keep in touch with the day centre and the informal carers on a day-to-day basis. The care manager monitors overall progress and tries to ensure that the allocated resources are used effectively and efficiently. The key worker and Mr Goldstein will review the objectives of the care plan in one month's time.

Mrs O'Neill

Mrs O'Neill is 82 years old and lives alone in a rambling five-bedroom house. She was widowed twelve years ago. A heavy smoker, she has developed chronic bronchitis which now severely limits her ability to carry out the cooking and cleaning. Following assessment, the care manager – in this case the field social worker – feels that sheltered accommodation might allow Mrs O'Neill to maintain much of her independence. She contacts the housing authorities to assist in the assessment. Mrs O'Neill is shown the kind of housing available, talks to the warden and is able to discuss what the change would mean. As a result, Mrs O'Neill is offered a sheltered flat and support from a community care worker (key worker) three days a week. The key worker reports back regularly on progress to the care manager.

After the first month Mrs O'Neill, the care manager and key worker discuss progress. Mrs O'Neill is coping better with practical tasks but finds it difficult to talk to neighbours. With Mrs O'Neill's agreement the key worker will discuss with the warden ways in which they can help Mrs O'Neill to increase her contacts with neighbours.

ACTIVITY

Discuss with colleagues and your supervisor the changes taking place in community care. These are large issues and you should return to them regularly – they cannot be dealt with easily or quickly. Some of the questions to keep in mind are:

- How does the National Health Service and Community Care Act try to improve arrangements for organising care?

- Who will represent the interests of the client?
- Will the changes improve services to the older person?
- How will the care manager fulfil his or her role?
- What will be the relationship between the care manager and the key worker?
- How can problems of communication be avoided?

3.4 Settings for care: *Domiciliary care*

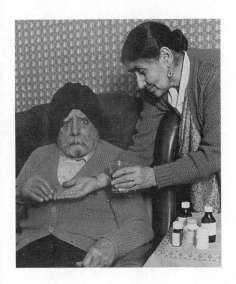

As earlier sections have shown, the vast majority of older people who require care in their own homes receive most of this from informal carers. The statistics confirm this clearly:

Care in the home (UK)
97% by informal carers
2.3% by social services departments
0.7% by the independent (i.e. voluntary and private) sector

However, for a variety of social, geographic, financial or personal reasons it is often impossible for informal carers to take on full responsibility for caring. They may live too far away, or have too little time because of work commitments. In other cases, there may be a poor emotional relationship between the client and relatives that prevents informal caring. There are also many changes in the client that make informal care difficult – for example, the development of severe physical disabilities or illnesses, incontinence and mental confusion.

Domiciliary services

Domiciliary care can take many forms, including:

- provision of meals;
- cleaning;

- shopping;
- companionship;
- monitoring and assessment;
- information-giving;
- day and/or night care;
- direct personal care, such as helping with bathing.

Many different facilities are involved in providing help and support in the home. As far as formal carers are concerned, job titles often vary from one employing authority to another. In addition to the specific tasks expected of them, all care workers can play a role in the general monitoring of the client's well-being. All regular visitors will also provide some degree of companionship. Domiciliary services include:

- *home helps* (home or community care assistants), who may assist with cleaning, ironing, washing, shopping and cooking;
- *meals-on-wheels services*;
- *community nurses*;
- *community therapists* (occupational therapists or physiotherapists, for instance);
- *social workers*;
- *health visitors*;
- various locally based schemes, usually voluntary, which might include:
  - *neighbourhood visiting schemes*, such as street 'wardens' who visit dependent or isolated people;
  - *lodgers* who provide an agreed amount of care;
  - *night sitters* to provide the main carer with much needed rest;
  - *'good neighbour' schemes*, sometimes directed towards the specific needs of clients from different ethnic origins, such as help with specialist diets.

The traditional home care service is gradually changing and focusing less on the domestic role of the care worker. Careful assessment allows domiciliary services to be directed more precisely towards what clients need most. Increasingly care workers need to take on the role of *advocate*: someone who is prepared to act with and for clients and their rights. This includes providing clients with information about welfare benefits and ensuring that problems are brought to the attention of the most appropriate person or department – so that solutions can be found promptly.

Care workers who work in the client's home must always realise that they are guests. Unlike their colleagues in residential care, there is no opportunity to fall back on the authority of the institution. Because of this, care workers need well-developed social skills to gain the trust of the client and to negotiate the kind of care that is acceptable. Many older people will find it difficult to adjust to the idea of a stranger coming into their home regularly to help with tasks which, until then, they have been carrying out for themselves. They may be fearful and suspicious. Pride and self-esteem take quite a knock in these circumstances and the last thing the client wants is a care worker who thinks she or he knows best. Some clients may also fear that accepting help of this type is inevitably the first step on the slippery slope leading to residential care.

Another dimension of care in the home is the link between care workers and informal carers, especially where the client is living with relatives. Careful negotiations may be necessary to sort out who does what. Like the client, informal carers may find it difficult to accept that they can no longer cope with the demands. To some outsiders, it may seem as if help of this kind should be welcomed with open arms. With human nature, however, it is rarely that simple, and all care workers should be aware of the pitfalls. Often a strong mutual dependence builds up between the carer and the person cared for, especially where the carers are relatives. There might also be young children or teenagers in the home. Although children and adolescents can be quite resilient, most will be going through mixed emotions of one sort or another – so the needs of all involved are important.

Visits will often serve more than one purpose. It is good practice to use visits to their maximum advantage by trying to be aware of the clients' general circumstances – don't concentrate solely on the main reason for the visit. Some of the points to keep in mind on each visit include:

- What contacts have clients had with their friends and relatives?
- How often are they managing to get out of the house?
- How many visitors have they had?
- Are they receiving and replying to letters regularly?
- Is the house reasonably clean and tidy?
- Are there unopened letters lying around?
- Are there any environmental hazards in the house, such as trailing leads, frayed wires, loose rugs or poor lighting?

As you get to know clients better, you can be more precise about what to look for.

Clients with different ethnic origins may experience particular problems over domiciliary care. Many will expect, with some justification, that they will be looked after by their relatives when frailty and sickness occur. However, not everyone will be so fortunate. Relatives may live a distance away; or a spouse may have died and there may be no children. Extra care must be taken in these circumstances to ensure that isolation does not become damaging.

In some parts of the country, efforts have been made to recruit home care staff from the ethnic groups represented by the clients. Certainly, care workers should be recruited from as wide a range of backgrounds as possible. Regardless of ethnic or other differences, *all* care workers should have as their goal the provision of genuinely individual care.

ACTIVITY

1 Select three clients who are receiving formal care in their own homes. Why is this care necessary? List your reasons under these headings:

- geographical;
- economic;
- personal.

If you are working in day or residential care settings, you will have to tackle this differently. Select three clients. Why are they unable to receive care at home? Use the same headings as above.

2 Discuss your responses with colleagues and your supervisor.

Reading on . . .

★ If you are interested in the multi-ethnic issues touched on in this section, you could investigate *Triple Jeopardy: growing old in a second homeland* by Alison Norman, published by the Centre for Policy on Ageing in 1985.

3.5 Settings for care: *Day care*

Most clients wish to stay in their own homes for as long as possible. But it is vital that this is combined with the chance to get out of the house regularly and to obtain help with basic care needs, such as diet and personal hygiene. Day care is one way in which these needs can be met, for example by providing a main meal, giving assistance with bathing, offering clients the chance to meet other people, and providing enjoyable and constructive activities.

Day care can be very flexible. It can meet a wide variety of needs without clients being cut off from their homes or communities, as might be the case with residential care. Day care can reflect the specific characteristics and needs of the local community. For instance, areas with a significant proportion of older people from different ethnic origins have established specialist voluntary day centres. These are often much more than places to meet: language teaching, advice on health, and specialist meals-on-wheels services have all been offered by such centres.

What are the advantages and disadvantages of day care?

Advantages

Day care has various clear advantages:

- Staff are usually close to the community and to the family support services (relatives, friends and neighbours).
- Day care offers a richer social life and a change of scene.
- Activities can be offered to informal carers, for example relatives' support groups.
- Day care offers respite to informal carers who otherwise would get no break.
- It can act as a resource base for informal carers and care workers, providing advice and guidance on a range of practical issues.
- It can be used as a communication channel for many different services. Depending on the nature of the day centre, professional social workers may be on hand to provide specialist support and guidance.

Disadvantages

However, day care also has certain possible disadvantages:

- It may be difficult to link day-care activities with the rest of the client's life. For example, skills being developed in the unit may not be easy to carry on in the client's own home.
- Some older people find it difficult to cope with the repeated shifts from one environment to another.
- The lack of continuity between the home and the day-care centre can cause problems. For example, clients may have been used to preparing certain of their meals at home. At some day centres, they may have to adapt to a more dependent role in which meals are prepared by someone else.

Alternative types of day care

Resource centres

The idea of the resource centre for older clients is becoming more popular. This offers 'drop-in' facilities where clients can meet their friends and relatives over a cup of coffee. A crèche for grandchildren might be available and social workers can assist with specialist needs.

Family care schemes

These are schemes in which day care is provided by informal carers in their own homes. Payment is made to the carers on a sessional basis. It can be a particularly useful scheme for people with confusion or dementia because the more restricted, homely environment is less muddling to the client and care can be more individual and specific. It's demanding work for the carers, however, and care staff need to provide support.

Implications for care workers

Links between home and day care

Consider carefully the links between home and day centre. Be aware of the problems of continuity and think of ways in which links can be made. Make sure that you ask clients to tell you about what's happened to them since you last saw them: don't just get on with the business of the day.

Helping clients to adjust

Watch carefully for signs that clients may be finding it difficult to make the rapid adjustment between home and centre. Try to prevent problems by making a point of greeting clients in a consistent way on each arrival and establishing a helpful routine.

Knowing the clients

Get to know the clients as well as you possibly can, taking a personal interest in each one.

How well you can get to know clients depends on the organisation of care in the centre. With large numbers of clients, some form of allocation of clients to care workers (the key worker system, for example) may be needed. In other cases, group activities can be used to develop closer relationships.

Recording care

The recording of care in day centres can be something of a challenge. Complicated systems of the kind used in residential care are often inappropriate in day care because of the shorter contact between staff and clients. Each centre will have its own approach. What is always important is to find a way for staff to record for the benefit of others the changes taking place in clients. Day care should have a positive purpose for clients and you need to be able to record progress. As far as possible, clients should be involved in this process and should be able to feel that they are actively engaged in a partnership with day-care staff.

3.6 Settings for care: *Residential care*

Residential care for older people has had a chequered history, both in the distant and more recent past. As a result, residential care has ended up with something of a stigma attached to it. Although very expensive to set up and run, it is often seen as a second-best service. And the staff involved very often suffer the same fate, being viewed as second-class professionals when compared to colleagues who work outside an institution.

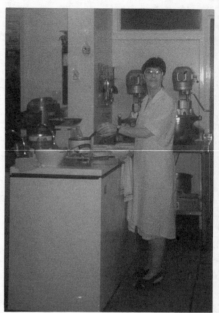

This negative attitude is very unfortunate and should be challenged at every opportunity. Clients are entitled to the kind of care that best suits their changing needs. For some, residential care is the best option. What matters is that the service, like every other, is offered only to people who really need it – and that need should be reviewed regularly.

There are several recent developments that have influenced residential care:

A 1985 Audit Commission report

Managing Services for the Elderly More Effectively raised concern over what the report saw as the inappropriate placement of older people into residential care; it said that there was poor coordination and weak overall management of the community services.

Growth in the private sector

Rapid growth of the private sector, especially since 19
residential care for older people. There was a particularl
1983 when DHSS benefit changes led to the government fu
specified level for different client groups. In the period from 1970 to 1987
the number of residential places for older clients in the private sector grew
from 23 700 to 127 900 – more than a five-fold increase. From 1979 to
1989 the number of people in independent residential care and nursing
homes – mostly older people – who were claiming income support (pre-
viously supplementary benefit) rose from 12 000 to 176 000.

The 1984 Registered Homes Act

This Act brought in measures to control standards within both care homes
and nursing homes. Care homes have to register if they offer both board and
personal care. 'Board' is the provision of food and accommodation;
'personal care' is roughly equivalent to what could be provided by a
competent and caring relative able to deal with emotional as well as physical
needs. Staff of care homes are not expected to provide professional health
care. That is the function of the primary health-care services. Residential
care homes are registered and inspected by the social services department;
nursing homes by the district health authority. A code of practice – *Home
Life* – was published in 1984.

The Act covers a wide range of aspects, including these:

- the suitability of the premises;
- the suitability of the applicant for registration;
- services and facilities;
- the management of care.

Each local authority interprets the Act and produces its own guidelines for
present and prospective home-owners. Registration can be refused or
withdrawn if homes do not meet the standards required. There are regular
inspections – announced and unannounced – and formal reports are written
on these visits.

The Wagner Report (1988)

A committee was commissioned by the government to look into residential
care. Chaired by Gillian Wagner, it published its report, *Residential Care: a
positive choice*, in 1988. Forty recommendations were made, covering
registration and inspection, staffing and training, and individual rights.
Many of these have found their way into subsequent legislation and have
influenced how local social services departments interpret these laws.

National Health Service and Community Care Act 1990

This is an enormously important piece of legislation, with profound
implications both for care in the community and for the national health
service. Homes run by social services departments now have to be inspected.
This should ensure that standards are the same throughout the country.
Inspection units have been established that are responsible for monitoring
standards in all sectors of residential care. Local authorities have to prepare,
publish and review plans for the provision of community care. The box on

s page shows how one local authority has established progressive aims for residential care that will form a part of its planning.

Local authority social services departments will increasingly buy services from the independent (private and voluntary) sector, rather than running their own services. Many authorities have begun to sell their homes for older people to private organisations.

Aims and objectives of residential care

To provide accommodation where sensitive and skilful care is available for people who, even with help, can no longer live in their own home.

The primary aim is to enable residents to live as normally as possible in a situation where their individuality, independence and personal dignity are respected. The best practice in residential care aims at a positive approach to residents' capabilities and at encouraging them to use their faculties to maintain their independence and enjoy their lives as fully as possible, maintaining and encouraging the possibility of returning to a home of their own or to some form of sheltered accommodation.

(Essex County Council, Social Services Department, April 1991)

Some local authorities have tried to implement aims such as these by establishing homes for particular groups. Birmingham, for example, opened a home specifically for Asian clients. It can offer care for Sikhs, Muslims and Hindus. Staff include Asian cooks and care workers who can speak the appropriate languages.

ACTIVITY

Many of the changes that have been made are quite controversial. They are very wide-ranging and have a host of social, economic and political implications. They will also create new roles and opportunities for care staff.

1 Talk to a number of people involved in residential care for older people. Ask them how they think things will change over the next few years. You might think of approaching some of the following people:

- a private-sector care home-owner or manager;
- a social worker;
- a representative from a local voluntary organisation, such as Age Concern;
- a manager of a local authority residential home.

How would you describe the differences between them in their views on this topic?

2 Discuss the exercise with your supervisor, who will be able to suggest the best way of proceeding locally – for example, who to approach for the necessary permission.

This is a large exercise and you might find it easier to carry out with colleagues.

Reading on . . .

★ *Home Life: a code of practice for residential care*, published in 1984 by the Centre for Policy on Ageing, has become an essential reference for many in the field. More recent publications include *Caring for Quality: guidance on standards for residential homes for elderly people* (Department of Health Social Services Inspectorate, 1990).

3.7 Settings for care: *Working in residential care*

Residential care is always something of a compromise. The home has to run smoothly and efficiently, and yet the staff have to provide care that is sensitive and individual. Blending these two requirements is not easy and cannot be achieved in a 'once and for all' way: care has to be worked at continuously.

The benefits of working in residential care

The advantages of working in residential care can easily be overlooked. Here are some of the most important:

- being part of a community is a need that many of us have – this may help to break down the barriers between clients and members of staff;
- working as part of an established team can be very rewarding, both professionally and personally;
- continuity of contact with clients allows staff to know the needs of the clients in great detail and means that trusting relationships can more easily be built up;
- standards of care can be under closer scrutiny than is often the case in other situations;
- the full 24 hours is available for the organisation of care – by contrast, only the working day (extended in various ways, perhaps) is available in domiciliary and day care.

However, these are benefits that have to be earned through constant vigilance. There are dangers in any institutional setting.

Becoming institutionalised

One of the main problems in residential care is *institutionalisation*. Although known about for decades, it remains one of the most difficult problems to deal with in any setting where people have to live most of their lives. It applies equally to long-stay hospitals, prisons and children's homes, and can affect staff as well as residents. Residents in care homes are especially vulnerable to institutionalisation because they may be less mobile and also, in some cases, less mentally able to assert themselves. Both of these conditions create an atmosphere of acceptance and conformity to routine.

How can you recognise institutionalisation in clients? These are some signs to watch for:

- apathy – very little motivation to do more than conform to the routine;
- withdrawal – no wish to communicate with others beyond what is absolutely necessary;
- reduced eye contact;
- few changes in facial expression;
- head bowed;
- the failure ever to argue or answer back – a simple acceptance of whatever happens.

The causes of the problem are diverse:

- staff attitudes – being rather bossy, even in a kindly way;
- a regime of care that is rigid and cannot respond to individual needs;
- an environment that is drab and institutional, with little opportunity for clients to make it their own;
- a closed rather than an open atmosphere, where few outside visitors are seen;
- a low level of stimulation, with very few activities on offer;
- no opportunities for residents to get out regularly;
- little privacy for residents.

Don't forget that there will always be particular individuals who are quieter and mix less. That's perfectly normal, of course. The time to worry is when the signs start to show themselves in the behaviour of *several* residents.

Preventing institutionalisation

It can be easy to confuse the effects of institutionalisation with some of the features of ageing itself. If the damaging effects of being in an institution are not appreciated, then the signs might even be misconstrued as being due to an irreversible condition such as dementia.

Make sure you know the signs of institutionalisation. Review your own attitudes from time to time, asking yourself questions like these:

- How many occasions are there when I put routine before the needs of the client? Am I sure that these are all absolutely necessary? (Don't be too worried if you do find yourself doing this from time to time – no one is perfect.)
- How do I respond when someone or something threatens to change my routine? (If it throws you into a panic, you yourself have probably started to become institutionalised. Try to prevent this reaction by regularly making changes in your own care practice.)

ACTIVITY

To some extent even the best residential homes show some of the features of institutionalisation. That's why it is a problem that can never be finally beaten.

List *three* changes that could be made to your own work setting that would make it less institutionalised.

ACTIVITY

Review the routine in your workplace. How often are changes made? When they are, are they for the benefit of the staff, or the residents, or both? Discuss your responses with colleagues and your supervisor.

3.8 Settings for care: *Integrated care*

So far, care settings have been described as if they existed only as separate entities. But this is not necessarily the case. Increasingly services are appearing that bring together a wide variety of different resources for the care of older clients. These facilities offer day care, sheltered accommodation, residential care and nursing care in a single location.

To date, most of these developments have come in the private and voluntary sectors. The inspiration for some of these has come from the USA, where the idea of the integrated facility for older people has been around for some time. Retirement communities have been created offering a lifestyle most appropriate to older people. Originally geared mainly to the needs of the healthy 'young-old' person, many are now catering specifically for clients needing care. Such places are referred to as 'continuing-care retirement communities' or 'life-care communities'. They combine independent living with a range of personal care and specialised nursing. The usual practice in the USA is for the client to pay an entrance fee, together with regular monthly payments according to the level of care required. Most have been set up by non-profit-making organisations or charitable trusts. Links with the local community are usually very positive, with clients sometimes participating in charity work.

In the UK, moves in this direction have been on a smaller scale. Cultural differences are significant: it is no use trying to foist an alien system on to an unwilling population. Although in this section it is the formally established communities that are being considered, it is worth remembering that there are many areas of the UK, often coastal resorts, which have become virtual retirement communities because of their popularity with retired people. Due to the influx of older people, services have grown in an attempt to meet the new priorities, resulting in the formation of unplanned retirement communities.

Future changes

The National Health Service and Community Care Act 1990 has set out major changes in the funding of community care. Local authorities will have responsibility for directing money to the most appropriate services, by purchasing these from providers on a contractual basis. They are being encouraged to make full use of the private and voluntary sectors. Because of this, private enterprise has diversified into new areas. In addition to providing residential care for older people, many have expanded into day care; various forms of flexible domiciliary care may be the next growth area.

These changes may mean that some older clients will have a greater choice in how they obtain their care. Care workers too will have to deal with a different set of working conditions. They may have to be much more flexible and adaptable, and possess skills that allow them to work in a variety of settings.

ACTIVITY

Look at the following lists. They suggest some of the ways in which care provision might change in the next few years.

Discuss these with your colleagues. Add to the lists if you think aspects are missing.

Present provision
- mainly separate facilities;
- large local authority sector, providing residential, day and domiciliary care;
- growing private sector, mainly providing residential care;
- few integrated facilities.

Future provision
- fewer separate facilities;
- small local authority sector, providing specialist, intensive services and purchasing the bulk of care from the independent sector – some existing social care services may be contracted out;
- many integrated services, such as:
  - residential care *plus* day care;
  - residential care *plus* day care *plus* domiciliary care;
  - day care *plus* domiciliary care;
  - residential care *plus* day care *plus* domiciliary care *plus* professional fieldwork.

ACTIVITY

You are working in a complex that has been purpose built for older clients. It covers several acres and contains the following facilities within its boundaries:

- a residential care home;
- a nursing home;
- sheltered accommodation;
- a 'village' with a few shops, a small cinema and banking facilities;

- a pleasant environment, including a lake, a large expanse of grass for easy walking, tennis courts and a putting green;
- transport arrangements to take residents to the nearest town (some twenty miles away) four times a week.

1 Choose three other services that you think should be available. What are your reasons for these choices?

2 What are the advantages and disadvantages of creating large complexes like this?

3 Do you think that this way of organising care should become the dominant one in this country?

4 Discuss your views with colleagues and your supervisor.

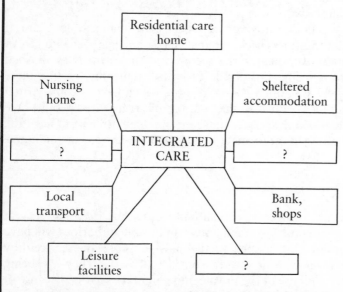

Formal caring involves structured planning and is
knowledge and skills. As a care worker, you need to u
involved in planning care so that you can participate in ......ed way.

Planning care rationally is a vital contribution to meeting the obligation
to provide clients with the highest possible standards. Although feelings and
intuition certainly have roles to play, caring benefits from a thoughtful and
organised approach.

Think of it this way. In setting out to buy the best car for your money,
you wouldn't dream of going into the garage and buying the first one that
caught your eye. You would probably sit down and make a few decisions
before getting anywhere near a garage. For example, you might think about
style, colour, size, make, price and so on. As a result, you would set yourself
some goals. Armed with these, you could then venture into the car
showrooms. Eventually, you would decide to buy. Having bought, you
would begin the process of judging whether or not you had made a wise
choice.

Planning for care is much more complex than this, of course, but the
analogy helps to identify some of the stages in the process.

Stages in planning

Care planning involves several stages. Later sections will describe each in
detail. These are the stages:

Assessment

This involves:

- gathering information about clients;
- assessing the needs, the problems and the strengths of the clients.

Goal-setting

This involves:

- deciding on appropriate targets for care;
- prioritising these targets.

Implementing care

This involves:

- selecting activities and approaches to care in order to achieve the goals
  set;
- carrying out these activities

Evaluating care

This involves:

- deciding whether goals have been achieved;
- making changes to the care plan in this light.

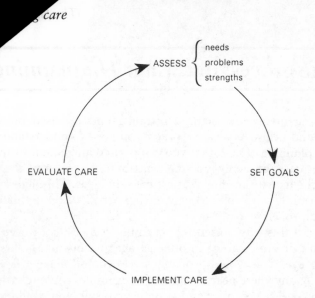

The diagram shows broadly how the stages relate to one another. Although it suggests that stages always follow each other in a particular order, this is an over-simplification. In practice, they overlap a great deal, each stage being to some extent a continuous activity.

Partnership and negotiation – involving clients

Partnership and negotiation are important aspects of care, and include:

- explaining about the process of care planning;
- asking for the clients' views on how they see their needs;
- agreeing goals for care;
- discussing ways in which goals can be met;
- deciding together how well goals have been achieved;
- deciding jointly what should happen next.

Clients have the right to be treated as partners in their care – relatives too, with the client's permission. Partnership and negotiation have to be interpreted for each client and each situation. There are many factors that should be considered in the course of trying to involve clients. How far do clients *want* to participate? It may take some time to encourage partnership. Many people are accustomed to remaining passive in the face of authority, even where the authority is responsible for providing care. It's a little like being a patient in hospital: many people *expect* to be powerless.

There are cultural and class differences that should be considered, as well. Language problems will make free communication and participation difficult. Some older Afro-Caribbeans and Asians may have suffered economic and social disadvantages because of their colour; some also from their earlier status as immigrants. Partnership means sharing private details with a care worker who is a virtual stranger, and this may be difficult for a sensitive client. At times care worker and client may not agree on aspects of care planning, such as what the needs are, what the goals should be or how to achieve them. In such cases, it is important for those organising the planning of care to be clear about how these differences of view are to be handled. When this happens, you should report such differences to your supervisor and record them in writing.

There will be times when partnership proves difficult to put into practice, such as when clients are confused or have other severe communication difficulties. Nevertheless, there are always ways in which some level of involvement can be achieved.

A *case study*

The value of thinking logically about care planning can be seen most clearly when things go wrong. A brief case study will make this clear:

> Because Mrs Cheng, a new admission, was unable to walk, the care staff decided to place her chair near to the window overlooking the garden. A day or so later, she started to become rather agitated. When her care was being evaluated with her relatives it became apparent that for many years she had been unable to tolerate bright light. The care workers had not discussed the likely pattern of her day with the relatives or with Mrs Cheng on admission, and so had missed this most important aspect of her care. A thorough initial assessment might have prevented the problem. Because there was prompt and systematic evaluation of Mrs Cheng's care, however, the problem was brought to light before too much damage had been done.

ACTIVITY

Care planning is a team activity. Discuss the following questions with colleagues and your supervisor.

- Are individual care plans discussed regularly?
- How well is the time spent at planning meetings? Does the team keep to the point? Is the chairperson or leader effective?

- Are all team members encouraged to contribute their ideas?
- How are differences of opinion resolved?

3.10 The caring process: *Assessing*

The assessment of care is a vital but complex process. It involves:

- collecting information;
- recording and reviewing information;
- interpreting information.

Whatever the care setting, information gathered about clients forms the basis of care planning. At its most basic this includes essential biographical data – for example, name, address, date of birth, marital status, religion, next-of-kin, health record. Although vital, this type of information is only a start. To be able to organise care that is sensitive, relevant and creative, care workers need to go well beyond this, to build a more comprehensive picture of the clients and their abilities, aspirations, perceptions and expectations. This will lead to an assessment of their care needs and the development of a care plan.

Reasons for assessment

These will vary considerably. At certain stages of the process, formal professional assessments by social workers, nurses or other professionals will be carried out so that the most beneficial setting for care may be offered. For example, a general practitioner may refer an older client to a day centre because she is concerned for his safety. (Perhaps the gas has been left on repeatedly and the neighbours are becoming concerned over the risk of fire.) Care workers may assist in this process but will not be expected to undertake it themselves.

In some circumstances, assessment may take place in the client's own home. Here, power is very much more in the hands of the client, and the care worker has to adopt the role of guest. Considerable experience is needed before effective assessments can be made in these situations. Consequently, it is likely that professionally qualified care workers would undertake these.

This section is mainly concerned with assessments that can be carried out by care workers under supervision.

Sources of information

To be useful, information must be accurate and relevant. Sources of information include:

- the client directly, through formal interviews, informal conversations and observations;
- relatives and friends of the client;
- professional colleagues, such as social workers and community nurses;
- documents, such as referral forms and previous assessment sheets.

How to assess

The first contact between care worker and client is particularly important. It is essential that you establish a relationship based on trust and mutual respect. If you are organised and well prepared you will create a sense of trust more easily than if you are rushed and ill prepared. Understandably, older clients may be wary of disclosing personal information. On the other hand, some clients may agree to answer questions too readily, especially when put by someone they see as being in authority. You must be prepared to act as an advocate for the client by being sensitive to the power that you wield while assessing.

The client should be made aware of the reasons for your asking particular questions, and should feel under no obligation to respond unless he or she sees a clear reason to. Effective assessment is based on good communication skills. (These are discussed in section 4.4.) Points to note when assessing are these:

- *Being comfortable* Make sure that both you and the client are comfortable, and that you are making eye contact at the same level – never look down at a client when talking.

- *Your role* Explain your role and why the assessment is necessary.

- *Language* Use appropriate language – avoid all professional jargon.

- *Questions* Choose appropriate types of question – for example, closed questions for factual information, open ones for opinions and feelings.

- *Observation* Observe carefully all aspects of the client's behaviour – what is said, how it is said, and what behaviour accompanies the words.

- *Recording* Keep to a minimum the amount of information you need to write down at the time of the interview.

- *Length of interview* Don't make the interview too long, as some clients may have difficulty concentrating – in these cases, spread the assessment over two or more sessions.

- *Checking* Before you finish, remember to check details with the client to ensure that you have heard correctly.

Where to assess

The place in which you assess the client matters for several reasons. Because of problems of hearing, vision or mental confusion, older people can find strange environments particularly difficult. If the setting for the assessment is inappropriate, the client may be unwilling to discuss personal matters. The information gathered will be incomplete or inaccurate and a potentially effective relationship may have been damaged. Make every effort to avoid this by getting the conditions right.

A hurried interview in a communal room shows a lack of respect for the client and indicates little forethought on the part of the care worker. In most cases, it should be possible for you to plan ahead and ensure that a quiet place – preferably a room for this purpose – is available. Ensure that your colleagues are aware you are there, so that you are not disturbed. If crises arise, it is better to postpone the formalities until things have settled down. Everyone will feel more relaxed later and a better job will be done.

When to assess

The exact time for a first assessment by the care worker needs careful thought. It is often better to introduce clients into a new situation gradually, allowing them to adjust at their own pace. Encouraging them to strike up a conversation with a fellow client is often helpful. Once this has been achieved, the formal aspects of the initial assessment can begin in a more relaxed atmosphere.

What to assess

It is important to use structured assessments so that care can be designed to meet specific needs. In response to this, some caring professions have devised extremely complicated frameworks for assessment. Any assessment system, however, will only be as good as the person using it. In the wrong hands, even the most sophisticated system can be clumsy and insensitive.

All types of assessment should try to deal with the whole person. Assessments should include how clients *feel* about their circumstances, rather than just concentrating on the details of their physical problems. However, information should not be collected for its own sake: this would be unethical as well as time-wasting. One problem is that, because older people have a lifetime of experience behind them, the assessment can draw upon large amounts of very varied information. Exactly what kind of information ought to be collected depends on several factors, for example how long the client will remain in the present care setting and how much is already known about the person. Details of what to assess will depend largely on the model for care used. (Models for care are considered in detail in section 3.11.)

ACTIVITY

1 Ask clients about their experiences of being assessed.

2 What did you learn which will help you when conducting future assessments?

ACTIVITY

1 Organise a role-play in which you act as a client being assessed for the first time. Ask a colleague to go through the types of questions you would normally ask a client. Note your reactions to this process.

2 Try repeating the exercise with variations – in a different place, with more or less noise, in a hurried or relaxed manner on the part of your colleague 'interviewer'.

3 Change roles so that you act as the interviewer.

4 Discuss your responses to these experiences with your supervisor. How did you feel acting as the client being assessed? Did any aspects cause you concern? As a result, can you suggest ways in which assessment could be improved in your own care setting?

3.11 The _____
for ca...

What is a mode...

'Models for care' may s...
uses models all the time. ...
consult a map. A map – sm...
features of a country. At t...
model. Nevertheless maps st...
model of care helps us to find ...
– directing us towards what we ...

In providing care, we use m... ...ne
care workers are excellent at seein... ...may find
dealing with psychological problem... ...gests that their
model shows clients as mainly co... ...al systems that need
correcting when they go wrong. By ... ...hers may see clients as in
need of social care; physical care might ... a lower priority. In either case, the
model will influence the actions and attitudes of the care worker.

Is this satisfactory when it comes to organising care for older clients?
Well, it might be. But it depends so much on the intuitive skills of whoever is
making the decisions. Most of us cannot rely on our feelings and instincts to
get things right first time, and so we have to depend to some degree on
outside help. The main purpose of a model for care is to enable you to
pinpoint the clients' most important care needs. This will allow you to help
develop a care plan with, as well as for, the client. Remember that, wherever
possible, the client should be in control and able to influence the care that is
being proposed – all models for care should have this principle at their core.
Where clients are unable to join in care planning, perhaps because of
confusion, you have to put yourself in the clients' place and try to see things
as they would see them.

Models can only be judged by how well they work in practice.

Types of model

Models for care present the process of caring in simplified form. Once this is
done, you then have a guide which indicates the most appropriate ways of
assessing, planning and carrying out care. Whatever model you use should
be consistent with your philosophy of care (see section 3.2).

Here are two kinds of model that can be used as starting points.

The 'human needs' model

This model is based on the belief that all clients share a set of needs that must
be satisfied. If clients cannot themselves meet some of these for whatever
reason, then care is required to help satisfy them. Old age is clearly one of
the reasons why some needs may go unmet; others include physical or
mental illness, or adverse circumstances.

Models of this kind are often derived from the work of the psychologist
Abraham Maslow who described human needs as being arranged in a
hierarchy, as shown in the diagram on page 40. The general principle is that
lower needs – such as physiological needs – must be satisfied before higher
needs. For instance, most people are more worried about getting adequate
food than they are about studying philosophy. However, not everyone fits

...to satisfy higher needs while
...artist who struggles to complete a
...y, or the bereaved person who shuns the
...o devote himself to the memory of his loved

...this model would be to assess and plan care using
...ut we need something more. One of the difficulties of
...needs model for care is that it can make us think just in terms
...acking. If we stick to this approach, we are inclined to think only
...lems and weaknesses. One means of avoiding this is for each need to
...assessed in terms of both strengths and weaknesses. So, an assessment
sheet might look like this:

Needs	Strengths	Weaknesses
Physiological		
Safety/security		
Love/belonging		
Self-esteem		
Self-actualisation		

One advantage of adapting well-established models such as this is that they have stood the test of time and they tend to take a broad view of human nature.

If you use this model as a basis for assessing care needs, you may find that physiological needs, such as eating and sleeping, are easier to recognise and record than psychological ones, such as self-esteem. For example:

- Physiological needs:
  - *Strength* Joseph can walk to the local shops without assistance.
  - *Weakness* He needs to get up three times in the night to go to the toilet.
- Self-esteem needs:
  - *Strength* Judith takes pride in the pleasure she gives others through her letter-writing.
  - *Weakness* She is concerned about her 'failure' to form satisfying relationships during her life.

However, with supervision and practice you will find that you can begin to recognise the full range of needs. Remember that, to keep your assessments as objective as possible, you should always discuss them with your supervisor.

'Activities of daily living' model

Another way of viewing care is to start with those activities that everyone needs to carry out every day: the activities of daily living. There is no one way of drawing up such a list and the ideas given here are only a suggestion. As always it is important for staff to discuss and agree what it is that works for them, to test it out with clients and to modify it as needed. A list of activities could look something like this:

- breathing;
- eating and drinking;
- eliminating (that is, passing urine and faeces);
- moving;
- dressing;
- sleeping;

- communicating and forming relationships;
- perceiving the environment – using the five senses;
- personal care – keeping clean and well groomed;
- avoiding dangers;
- motivating self – interests, leisure, driving forces;
- expressing sexuality;
- spiritual needs, including attitudes to death.

Again, if you use this approach for assessment, you could look for both strengths and weaknesses.

ACTIVITY

1 Think about the Maslow hierarchy of needs.

- Can you think of ways in which you don't fit into that model? Are all your needs represented there?
- Can you think of clients who seem not to follow this general pattern?

2 Discuss your responses with colleagues and your supervisor.

ACTIVITY

Consider in turn each of the activities of daily living.

- How would you go about trying to assess these?
- The model gives only very broad headings. Ask yourself what exactly is meant by each one. Try to subdivide them so that they become clearer.

- Are there any categories that you would like to add?
- What about clients receiving care in their own homes? Should there be more opportunity to assess clients' social circumstances? Add categories as you see fit. What matters is that it should work for the client and care team.

Maslow's 'human needs' hierarchy

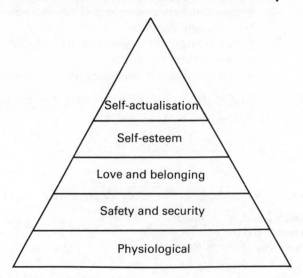

Self-actualisation:	To become all that we are capable of becoming – to reach our full potential.
Self-esteem:	To respect, and feel pride in, ourselves.
Love and belonging:	To want companionship and personal relationships. To wish to feel part of the community.
Safety and security:	To live in a safe environment, free from hazards. To be materially and financially secure.
Physiological:	To survive – through being able to eat, to drink, to breathe, to sleep, to stay warm, to have sex (species survival).

Reading on . . .

The ideas in this section owe a good deal to theories developed in the nursing field. There are several interesting nursing textbooks that you might like to look at if you wish to extend your knowledge of models. Don't be put off by the word 'nursing' in the titles: those recommended here can quite easily be adapted to the care – rather than nursing – of the older person.

★   Alan Pearson and Barbara Vaughan: *Nursing Models for Practice*, published in 1986 by Heinemann. This is a clearly written textbook which is also good to look at. It covers several different models and includes examples of how to put them into practice.

★   Christine Chapman: *Theory of Nursing: practical application*, published in 1985 by Harper & Row. Despite its rather daunting title, this is a short introductory textbook which explains complicated ideas very clearly.

★   Peter Aggleton and Helen Chalmers: *Nursing Models and the Nursing Process*, published in 1986 by Macmillan Education. Although covering much of the same ground as the books mentioned above, it also shows how the 'nursing process' helps nurses to organise their nursing care. This is similar to the 'care process' described in section 3.9.

3.12 The caring process: *Setting go*

Once an assessment of the client's needs has been made, the next step should be to decide on appropriate goals. Some people use the term 'aim' or 'objective' instead of goal. It doesn't matter which word is used. What does matter is to understand the importance of this stage in the process of caring. Without clear goals care cannot be organised rationally.

What is a goal?

A *goal* is a statement of the behaviour that a client should be able to achieve after a certain period. For example:

> *Goal* Eamon will be able to show you where his room is, within seven days after admission.

The reason that the word 'behaviour' is used is that it helps to define the *results* of care. It is not without its problems, however. The example given here is fairly straightforward. What if you want to set a goal that is more complicated? Here is an example concerned with psychological care:

> *Goal* Rezia will feel less unhappy about having to accept day care. She will start to join in organised social activities within one month.

Where clients are suffering from psychological stresses, it is more difficult to set clear goals. Obvious questions are, what does 'feel less unhappy' mean? And can we assume that, by 'joining in', she is becoming less unhappy? Perhaps not. So you might want to qualify some of these statements to make your meaning clearer. But there is a limit to this: you will never be able to solve every problem when setting goals. Yet if no goals are set, how will you know whether any progress is being made?

Setting goals

Goals should be set through discussion with the client and the care team on the basis of the assessment of the client's needs. This activity should be a joint one involving a range of people as necessary – for example, a

physiotherapist for mobility problems or a continence advisor when the client cannot keep dry. Occasionally, clients may not be able to contribute to this process because of illness, either physical or mental. In most cases, however, they are able to play some part. You will make this easier if you try to reduce care-planning jargon to a minimum. In fact, the use of jargon of any kind is usually unhelpful, even between colleagues.

Goals should be:

- realistic;
- achievable;
- observable;
- measurable.

The first three of these are relatively easy to deal with: they are a matter of sensible decision-making, discussion and clarification. But what is meant by 'measurable'? Ideally, it should be possible to choose goals that can be measured. However, as we have seen, there are some goals that deal with areas of human behaviour that are more tricky, such as psychological care. No one has yet discovered a single, reliable means of measuring another person's state of mind that is useful in organising care. Nevertheless, every care worker has something to offer here and, through discussion between the client and the care team, it is often possible to arrive at psychological care goals that are observable and have meaning for all concerned.

Writing goals

Wherever possible, try to write goals from the client's point of view. Describe in simple language how you would expect the client to feel or behave differently to show that the goal had been achieved. The goals given so far as examples are worded in this way. Often, however, poorly worded goals are expressed in terms of the care worker's behaviour. For example:

Goal The care worker will help Eamon with walking every morning and evening.

This is not so much a goal of care as the means by which a goal might be achieved. Goals are ends, not means.

Prioritising goals

Not all goals are equally important. The number can be reduced by asking 'Which goals are the most important?' Depending on circumstances, it is often possible to select three or four goals that are most urgent.

Another way of reducing the task to a manageable level is to divide goals into short-term and long-term goals. Quite reasonably, some goals can be expected to be achieved over a period of days or weeks, rather than months or years.

3.13 The caring process: *Implementing care*

Having assessed clients' needs and set goals, the next phase is to organise the actual care. Different care settings will use different approaches. Several factors are important in deciding the approach:

Duration of stay

A client attending a day centre once a week, for example, is in quite a different position from another who is in semi-permanent residential care.

Size of establishment

A care home with fifty residents will need to use systems of care that are very different from those appropriate in a home for five. In a small home, care workers can get to know all residents well. This is not possible in a larger establishment – a different way of organising care is needed.

Clients' needs

Clients vary greatly in their needs. The more dependent clients are, the more intensive the care needs to be.

Types of care

Care can be divided into three kinds:

- doing *for* the client;
- doing *with* the client;
- *educating* the client.

Here are a few examples of these.

Doing for

The care worker puts shoes on the client's feet, laces them and makes sure that the client is comfortable. Physical or psychological disabilities may make this necessary. Nevertheless, the client must always be involved – by choosing which shoes to wear, for example.

Doing with

The client is able to put on his shirt but needs a care worker to fasten the buttons. In this case, there is no need for the member of staff to undertake all of the tasks. It is only necessary to carry out those the client cannot manage.

Educating

The care worker explains the importance of eating a diet with reduced carbohydrate. Once clients understand the significance of a healthy diet, they are in a better position to improve their own diets, if they wish.

The aim should be to do for the client *only* those tasks that are completely outside his or her range of abilities. Some care workers find this difficult. They would prefer to do more things for the clients, because they do not like to see them struggling, or perhaps because the clients take longer on their own than they would with help. However, becoming independent in even the most apparently simple tasks is a great achievement for many clients. Care workers will sometimes need to restrain themselves from interfering too much. As a care worker you should never take the clients' abilities for granted; rather, you should do all you can to encourage your clients to be independent.

How to organise care

There is no one right way of organising care. There are some important principles, however, that any system should try to embody. Here are three:

- *personal responsibility* – individual responsibility can improve motivation and commitment;
- *individual care* – to satisfy individual needs;
- *continuity of care* – good care must still be provided when staff change.

From the client's point of view what matters is that his or her needs are met in as personal and sympathetic a way as possible. There is no one way of arranging work to guarantee this. Some popular methods are as follows.

Key worker

In residential and day care, it can be useful to allocate to one care worker the responsibility for the care of one particular client for an extended period. Depending on circumstances, this may need to be a professionally qualified care worker or a senior care assistant; it depends on the level of responsibility involved and the nature of the tasks.

Team approaches

In this approach, teams of care workers – each normally under the supervision of a senior care worker – are responsible for groups of clients. In this way, clients get to know a small number of care workers quite well. Responsibility is shared and this helps to ensure that care is consistent even when some team members are away.

Traditionally, care has tended to be linked to tasks: the need to undertake a particular task – for example serving meals – has outweighed the specific needs of individual clients, such as being able to observe carefully what a particular client is managing to eat. In some circumstances there are tasks that simply have to be done – perhaps making beds in a residential care home – and the quicker they are completed the sooner staff can direct their energies to the needs of individual clients. Allocating specific care workers to this one task might be justified, but it should not be the pattern for all care.

Supervision

Caring for others is stressful. One way of relieving some of these stresses, and providing helpful support, is to provide support for care workers. This is often called *supervision*, and entails regular meetings between the care worker and another person in the organisation who is able to offer advice, counselling and guidance on matters connected with caring. Discussion might range from problems over a particular client to personal difficulties about some aspect of caring. Not all care settings have yet established such supportive opportunities for their care staff but it will become increasingly necessary as the role of the care worker grows more demanding.

Support for informal carers

Section 3.1 shows how important informal carers are in helping older people in the community. When clients come into care the role of informal carers can seem to be less important. Where informal carers are able and willing to participate in caring, this should always be encouraged. In some cultures, relatives may expect to take a very active role in providing care for the client. Care workers should try to assess expectations of this kind early on in the process of planning care.

Planning care for a client should always include the role of informal carers and others of significance to the client. However, all care workers must recognise the stresses that informal carers are under and do all they can to provide support. Sometimes this takes the form of carer support groups – in a day centre or care home, perhaps. Different carers will have different needs. Some will still be caring for a relative at home and need practical advice on how to deal with problems or whom to contact if they can't cope. Others may no longer be giving much practical care – their relative might now be in residential care – but they may need to be able to talk about their feelings. Almost always, informal carers will benefit from the chance to meet others with similar experiences.

ACTIVITY

1 Examine the organisation of care in your own place of work or placement. How would you describe it, using the ideas expressed in this section – for example, key worker or team? In your view, are there ways in which it could be improved?

2 What do you understand by the term 'supervision'? What kind of supervision do you think would best meet your own needs?

3.14 The caring process: *Reviewing and evaluating care*

Reviewing and evaluating care are processes that help you to judge whether the goals of care have been achieved. At the time you set goals, think carefully about how you will decide later whether they have been met. Questions to keep in mind are:

When?

When should evaluation take place? Some goals might need daily evaluation, others once every six months: you will need to choose different review dates.

How?

How should evaluation take place? Informally or formally? Can special charts be used? Will evaluation be included as part of the usual records, in a diary or logbook, or should there be separate entries for the evaluation of each goal?

Who?

Who should carry out the evaluation? The key worker with the client, or the whole team? Will relatives be involved? And so on.

A case study

An example may help to make this clear.

> *Goal* Eamon will be able to show you where his room is, within seven days after admission.

- *When?* The timescale is clear – the goal should be achieved within seven days. Evaluation then needs to take place within this period. The goal may be achieved at an earlier stage, however, in which case it can be removed from the plan. When a goal is first written it is good practice to establish a *review date*. This ensures that it is not neglected. The date chosen is a matter of judgement and depends on the type of goal in question – whether short- or long-term, for example.

- *How?* But just what do we expect Eamon to have to do to meet this goal? Should he respond to a direct request, in rather a formal way? Or should we make use of the spontaneous everyday events in the home? This is not a clear-cut choice. Generally, the informal approach will be fine. It might be, however, that Eamon is following a programme of reality orientation that requires a more formal evaluation.

- *Who?* Eamon receives regular visits from his daughter and her husband. They are very concerned about him and wish to be involved in his care. In this case, it would make sense to bring them into the process of care planning from the outset. Eamon is mentally confused and has a strong Irish accent. His relatives can help care workers to understand him, so making the evaluation of his care more effective.

What do you do if the goal has not been achieved?

This occurs frequently and should not be seen as failure. Care planning is about people and so is a dynamic process, full of uncertainty. Each element in the process is constantly changing and so we should not expect it to run smoothly like a factory production line. These are some of the areas to consider when goals are not achieved:

- Was the goal *partly* achieved? Perhaps more time is needed.
- Was this goal necessary at all?
- Was the goal worded clearly so that it could be understood by all care workers?
- Was appropriate care offered? Are there other, better ways of achieving the same goal?
- Should the client be reassessed?
- Has the client's condition changed since the goal was originally set – has he or she been ill or bereaved, for example?

Possible outcomes from this review might be:

- to continue as before, allowing more time;
- to keep the goal, but try a different kind of care implementation;
- to change the goal, completely or in part;
- to reassess the client.

A general format for recording care

Client's name ....   Date ....

ASSESSMENT   Signature ....

Need/activity of daily living	Strengths	Weaknesses
....	....	....
....	....	....
....	....	....

Goals	Implementation	Review date	Evaluation
1			
2			
3			

A continence chart

	AM													PM									
	9	10	11	12	1	2	3	4	5	6	7	8	9	10	11	12	1	2	3	4	5	6	7	8
MON																								
TUE																								
WED																								
THU																								
FRI																								
SAT																								
SUN																								

Recordings can be by letter, e.g. w = 'wet', 'OK' if went to the toilet normally.

As with every stage of the care-planning process, evaluations should be recorded accurately. The examples of care-plan documents given here may stimulate you to think of other even more effective methods.

ACTIVITY

1 How is care recorded in your present work setting? What would you say are its strengths and weaknesses? Discuss your ideas with your supervisor and colleagues. As a group, can you suggest ways of making improvements?

2 It is useful to compare different examples of care records. Discuss with your supervisor how you could go about this.

ACTIVITY

Sometimes it is helpful to design special 'evaluation tools' to keep a check on the progress of clients. The chart for recording when a client passes urine or is incontinent is one example.

1 Together with your colleagues discuss how you could create forms for recording a client's progress with respect to the following:

- dressing ability – how well the client is able to dress herself;
- diet – how much the client is eating and drinking;
- pain – how much pain the client is experiencing.

2 When you have some ideas, discuss them with your supervisor and try to assess their strengths and weaknesses.

A periodic progress review is suitable for longer-term care. It allows you to summarise progress and make suggestions for future action.

RESIDENT PROGRESS REVIEW

Name of resident: ....

Date of review: ....   Date of last review: ....

Participants in this review: ....

....

Summary of progress: ....

....

....

....

....

Targets for the next review period: ....

....

....

....

Suggested date for next review: ....

Signature: ....   Date: ....

Position:..

3.15   The caring process: *Reporting and recording care*

As earlier sections have shown, effective care planning needs an accurate system of reporting and recording which allows information to be stored and communicated.

Certain records must be kept by law. For example, care homes in the private and voluntary sectors, covered by the Registered Homes Act 1984, need to ensure that their records include the following:

- the aims and objectives of the home;
- for each resident, the client's name, address, date of birth, marital status, details of next-of-kin, details of the client's medical practitioner and social worker, the date of admission and of discharge, and details of who arranged the client's admission;
- for each resident, the case record: the client's special needs, medical treatment and progress reviews;
- medicines kept, administered and disposed of;
- accounts of any daily occurrences, and staff handover details;
- visits by authorised persons;
- food provided for residents;
- fire practices, drills or fire-alarm tests;
- the procedure to be followed in the event of fire, accidents or missing residents;
- people employed at the home;
- facilities provided in the home;
- money or valuables deposited by a residents.

The National Health Service and Community Care Act 1990 requires that all residential care homes, whether in the statutory or independent sectors, be regularly inspected. Each local authority has an inspection unit for this purpose. On each visit, the inspector examines how well records are kept.

Confidentiality

Clients entrust a great deal of personal information to care workers. In return staff must make every effort to ensure that this trust is not abused in any way. You must help protect the interests of clients by:

- not passing on information read in reports to other people who are not entitled to it;
- taking care not to discuss clients outside of the work setting;
- not discussing one client with another.

Principles of good recording

Precision

Care workers should aim to make their reports as precise as possible so that colleagues and other professionals who will read them are in no doubt as to their meaning. Records can also be used in the event of a complaint being made by a resident, relative or another member of staff, and so it is important that they are as accurate as possible.

Clarity

Records should be clearly and simply expressed. Avoid jargon and a very brief, note-form style. Write in clear, everyday language that everyone can understand, using complete sentences. For example:

> Mrs Kahn joined in with the others during the social skills group, saying how important it was to 'make an effort'.

is more helpful than

> Mrs Kahn met the initial objectives of the social skills group.

Choosing the right words

There are some simple ways of making your meaning clear. For example:

- use familiar rather than unfamiliar words;
- use short words rather than long;
- keep technical words to a minimum;
- keep sentences short;
- keep paragraphs short;
- use the active rather than the passive – 'I told Ms Mukerjee that her father had died' rather than 'Ms Mukerjee was informed of her father's death' – to make clear *who* took the action described;
- don't forget who is going to read your report – write for your next reader.

Objectivity

Avoid comments that are too subjective. Try to be as objective as possible by describing what actually happened, rather than your own view of events. Remember, though, that there is no such thing as an absolutely objective comment. Every observation is to some extent influenced by our own attitudes.

Verbatim reporting

The actual words spoken by the client are often of more use than interpretations made by staff. They convey better a sense of the client's real experience.

Data Protection Act 1984

Information stored on computer about identifiable, living people is controlled by this Act. Organisations that hold information on computer must apply to the Data Protection Registrar to be registered as data users. There are various data protection principles that must be complied with. These principles set out good practice in the use of computerised information.

Individuals are entitled to access to the information held about them on computer. However, where the information might cause serious harm to the individual's physical or mental health, it must not be disclosed. Advice must always be sought from an appropriate professional person, such as the client's general practitioner. Although this Act does not apply to record systems that are manual, rather than computerised, the principles concerning accuracy, confidentiality and security should be followed with any record system, as a matter of good practice.

ACTIVITY

Each care setting should have policies covering the kinds of information that should be reported and recorded. Do you know what these are? Are there areas that you are not sure about? If so discuss these with your supervisor.

Recent legislation covering health records has extended rights of access to manual information systems too: any patient now has the right to see his or her own medical records.

ACTIVITY

1 There are many dilemmas in the care worker's role. The area of confidentiality can be one. Can you think of any examples where you were uncertain whether to 'break a confidence'?

2 A relative approaches you and says: 'There is something I should like to tell you about my father, but first you must promise not to tell anyone else.' How would you respond to this? What are the reasons for your answer? Discuss your response with colleagues and your supervisor.

3.16 Moving into residential care: *Principles of good practice*

Coming into care

Clients make use of the caring services in many different ways. They may receive care at home; they may use the facilities of a day centre. But the most profound change that the older person has to make is the move into residential care; all other kinds of care leave clients relatively independent. However sympathetic and unobtrusive the regime is, a care home will to some extent lessen the independence of the individual client.

The first question to ask is whether such a move is necessary. Professionally qualified care staff, such as social workers, are normally responsible for helping clients to decide whether residential care is appropriate and acceptable. What criteria do they use? The National Institute for Social Work published a practical guide for *Assessing Elderly People for Residential Care*. Several key headings were suggested for the assessment:

- Problems: who is expressing a problem and about what? Are there conflicting views?
- Household composition: what are the current household circumstances of the older person? How does the client's disability affect his or her ability to cope?
- Physical disabilities and illness.
- Self-care ability: getting-up, preparing food, going to the toilet, answering the door, getting out and about.
- Confusion: for example disorientation.
- Risk: for example of accidents, fire and falls.
- The pattern of daily activity.
- Accommodation and environment.
- Informal carers and their problems.
- Decision-making: does the client know the importance of the decision? Does the client know and understand what residential care will be like?
- How important are very recent circumstances? Is the decision over residential care influenced by recent traumas?
- How does the client feel about the quality of his or her life now?

For many older people, deciding whether or not to enter residential care will be one of the most important decisions that they will ever have to make.

Their hopes and expectations will depend to a large extent on the accuracy of the assessment.

Although care workers are unlikely to be directly responsible for helping clients at this stage of decision-making, they will certainly have to deal with the consequences. They will need to support clients who are trying to come to terms with the pain of losing their familiar surroundings and a large part of their independence.

Care home managers and social workers go to great lengths to make the process as smooth as possible. Information is made available about the home so that prospective residents can see what facilities it has. Visits are encouraged before a final decision is made. In addition, when admission does finally take place it is usually on a trial basis. This lets the resident experience the home for a short period before reaching a final decision about whether to move in.

The process of admission

What should you consider when admitting a client for the first time?

- *Admission is stressful* This is likely however well organised the assessment and preparation. Moving from one environment to another involves losing what is known and having to cope with the unknown. If you've ever moved house, you'll know this – think how much harder it must be to move into a care home.

- *Admission means loss of control* Admission to a residential home always involves some increase in dependence. The sooner this is acknowledged, the sooner ways can be found to counteract its damaging effects.

- *Admission takes time to adjust to* It is easy to forget how difficult it can be for clients to absorb a new situation and new information. Put yourself in the client's position: remember that a strange place is difficult to cope with. A client can easily forget what you say on admission. You should always follow up the information given at this time with a later session. Some homes give new clients a specially prepared information pack.

Although these points are made with residential care particularly in mind, they can apply to day care, although to a lesser extent.

Principles of good practice

The process of admission can be rather bureaucratic: form-filling, dealing with property, giving factual information and so on. Each care home will have its own particular admission procedures that care workers will have to conform to. However, there are principles of good practice that apply in every case and help to make the process as straightforward as possible:

- *First impressions count* What takes place between care worker and client during admission is the start of a relationship, not simply a routine to be carried out.

- *Provide quiet and privacy* Choose a suitable environment for the initial talk – somewhere private and quiet.

- *Observe your client* Admission is the first step in assessment. It is important to be observant. Listen attentively.

- *Don't rush* Older clients may take longer to adapt to change.

- *Give new information over a period* To give too much too soon is a mistake. Decide what must be said on admission and stick to that – the rest can wait until later.
- *Arrange the next meeting* At the end of the meeting tell the client when you will be seeing him or her again.

Reassurance

Clients must feel secure and safe during admission. This means providing reassurance. But what exactly is reassurance? How can it be provided during admission?

- *Explain what is happening* Provide information as a response to questions, whether spoken or unspoken. Anticipate what the client might want to ask, and try to provide an answer.
- *Make familiar an unfamiliar situation* Introduce other clients and members of staff and show clients the main features of the care home. Avoid overwhelming clients by trying to include everything at once.
- *Introduce familiar experiences* For example, ensure that the client is able to bring personal possessions into the home, or make sure that familiar people (usually relatives) are present when admission takes place.
- *Stay calm* Be organised and handle sensitively what is always a difficult situation.
- *Allow the clients to talk about any fears or anxieties* This means helping clients to express emotions as and when appropriate.
- *Be professional* During admission client and care worker normally meet as strangers. In these circumstances it is important for you to allow the client some distance. Don't be too familiar too quickly. In particular, don't jump to the conclusion that it's all right to use a client's forename. Ask the client how he or she would prefer to be addressed.

ACTIVITY

1 Imagine yourself to be 80 years old. You have just decided to go into residential care. Draw up a 'balance sheet' of losses and gains, like this:

Losses	Gains
....	....
....	....
....	....
....	....

2 Discuss your personal balance sheet with a colleague. What does this exercise tell you about your attitudes towards residential care? What does it tell you about yourself?

Reading on . . .

★ The checklist at the start of this section is based on *Assessing Elderly People for Residential Care: a practical guide* by June Neill, published in 1989 by the National Institute for Social Work. This guide is clearly written and down-to-earth in its style.

3.17 Moving into residential care: *A case study*

This section consists entirely of a case study. It will help you to think about the areas you need to consider when a new client is about to come into care.

Read it through fairly quickly at first to get a general idea of what it's about. Look carefully at the questions, then read the case study again more thoroughly with these questions in mind. Finally, answer the questions as accurately as you can. If you can, do this exercise with your colleagues.

Miss Barbara Martin

The client, Miss Barbara Martin, is to be admitted to Beech Lodge, a private care home where you have worked for the past eighteen months as a care assistant. Beech Lodge has twenty-four residents – fifteen women and nine men – between 73 and 95 years of age. Three residents are significantly mentally confused but the majority have no mental disability other than mild memory problems. The home has a very pleasant garden overlooking the Yorkshire Dales.

The manager of the home has called a staff meeting to discuss Miss Martin's admission. You have been asked to take on the key-worker role. The manager gives you some relevant background information:

'She is coming up to her 83rd birthday – the week after next, in fact. Until she was 75, she worked as a music teacher, in schools at first but after retirement as a private teacher for local kids. Until she turned 70 she was really healthy but then she developed bad arthritis in her knees, hips . . . and her wrists. Over the past two years she's begun to suffer from chronic heart failure, too. This makes her breathless when she tries to walk more than a few yards. She's intelligent and has a good understanding of her medical conditions and drugs. Understandably, her illnesses are beginning to get her down.

On the personal side of things, she's never married and, according to her social worker, has only had a few close relationships in her life. As far as we know, her next-of-kin is a cousin she hasn't seen for some years.

She was an only child brought up in a working-class area not far from here. She learnt to be tough and self-reliant from an early age. Because of her musical talents, she got a scholarship to the local music college. She passed all her exams, including a music degree, and qualified as a teacher. For the past five years home has been a sheltered flat on the outskirts of town. Recently, she has found this too much to cope with. She realises that things cannot go on as they are for much longer. She knows she needs more help, but not too much. She came to visit last week. She only wanted to spend an hour or so here but she was happy to give it a try.'

As the key worker, you will have particular responsibilities for Miss Martin's care. You have just listened to the manager outline Miss Martin's circumstances.

ACTIVITY

1   The manager has told you that Miss Martin has visited Beech Lodge already. What information would you expect Miss Martin to have received *before* this initial visit, and who would have given her this information?

2   Miss Martin is due to arrive tomorrow morning at 10 o'clock. You have been asked to meet her, settle her in, and carry out the necessary administrative tasks.

- How will you prepare yourself for meeting Miss Martin?
- What will be your priorities for this first meeting? In order of priority, make a list of your aims in admitting Miss Martin.

3   Beech Lodge has just introduced a care-planning system based on Maslow's hierarchy of needs. You are expected to begin the assessment process.

- Knowing what you do about Miss Martin, what would you say were Miss Martin's areas of need? Try to suggest how her needs might fit into the Maslow framework, by completing the following table.

Self-actualisation needs: ....

Self-esteem needs: ....

Love and belonging needs: ....

Safety and security needs: ....

Physiological needs: ....

- What would you say are Miss Martin's strengths and weaknesses?
- When and how would you explain the idea of care planning to Miss Martin?

4   The initial stage of admission is over, including the administrative aspects.

- How would you expect Miss Martin to feel if you have been successful at this stage?
- What are your aims for Miss Martin over the next few days?

5   Compare your responses with those of your colleagues and discuss them with your supervisor. What *three* main lessons have you learned from this case study exercise?

3.18 Moving out of care

The possibility of moving on from one kind of care setting to another should always be kept in mind. As with admission, the most significant moves usually involve residential care – from residential care back to home, or to day care, for example. Even when it is day care that is coming to an end, getting used to being at home full-time can have its problems for both the client and his or her relatives.

Planning for discharge

The need for care planning is just as great in the build-up to discharge as it is at any other time. Despite this it is sometimes carried out rather hurriedly, if at all. As a result, it is all too easy for things to go wrong.

Planning for discharge should be based on a thorough, up-to-date assessment of the client's needs, strengths and weaknesses. The need to bring clients and relatives into planning is shown most clearly at this stage. Without their cooperation, plans may well be unrealistic or irrelevant. Under the new arrangements for community care, the care manager and key worker will need to ensure that there are effective channels of communication between the different parts of the care services. Because of this, discharge planning needs to be given a higher priority than it has so far achieved, to ensure that all agencies involved – for example social services, the family doctor and the community nurse – are prepared for the move.

Where possible, care workers who will be involved with clients after discharge should be drawn into planning and decision-making. Local policies will differ on this, but clients will usually find it reassuring to meet those care workers who will be seeing them later.

Preparing the client

Feelings about the move

Clients may well feel insecure at having to leave what has become familiar territory. But although new demands can be especially difficult for older clients, this is not always the case. For some, a fresh situation is a welcome challenge. Where a client is returning home after a spell in residential care, the extra demands may be very welcome.

In some cases, clients may have become rather institutionalised and might find the prospect of discharge frightening. Even where this is not the case, the idea of losing friends can be unpleasant.

Keeping in touch

The move can be made easier by discussing with clients ways that they can keep in touch. Care workers might be able to visit discharged clients from time to time, or clients could be invited back, perhaps on special occasions such as religious festivals or the birthday celebration of an old friend.

Planning a routine

Opportunities should be given for clients to think about how they are going to spend their time after discharge. Deciding on a routine ahead of the event can be both reassuring and of practical value. For clients whose memories are less than perfect, it is a good idea to prepare a timetable of routine activities for the week. Copies can be made for relatives and the care workers who will be responsible for follow-up visits.

Stress

Change always results in stress and this needs to be recognised. Older clients can be over-confident of their ability to cope. They can remember earlier times when they could manage perfectly well and may find it difficult to accept their present limitations. As a care worker, you will have to approach this issue with tact and sensitivity. The client will have to realise for herself that personal circumstances have changed, but you can do all you can to help reduce the pain of this.

Working with relatives

Relatives will share many of the client's worries. How will they readjust? Will a move be too demanding? What happens if things go wrong? What if they can't cope? If relatives are brought into the discussions at an early stage, these questions can begin to be answered.

The relatives' involvement will vary considerably according to individual circumstances. Some will need a good deal of support themselves; many may have to cope with problems and disabilities of their own. Relatives' support groups can be very helpful and are becoming more common.

A case study

The following case study will give you the chance to test your understanding of the ideas in this section and of care planning in general.

Mrs Amy Braithwaite

Amy Braithwaite, now just 75, came to this country from Barbados in 1957. She is married to Wesley, and they have four children. Three are married with their own children and live some distance away. One unmarried daughter still lives at home. These are her only relatives in this country, although she has two younger brothers in Barbados. The family live in a two-bedroom council house in an area of London with a high proportion of West Indians in the population.

For the past two years her memory has been gradually deteriorating. The family were able to cope with this until a few months ago when she developed mild pneumonia. This caused her to become confused and incontinent. Although treatment was quite effective, her illness left the family totally exhausted and Amy with even more memory difficulties. As a result she agreed to be admitted to a social services residential home for respite care and assessment.

Amy was allocated to a key worker while in the care home. This helped her to settle in quite quickly. Her amiable manner quickly made her popular with care workers and other clients. The main problem was her increasingly poor memory. She was able to talk at length about the past. Her childhood recollections were vivid and entertaining. The only problem was that, within minutes, she had totally forgotten who she had told what, and so every care worker heard a similar tale many, many times.

During her stay she had been involved in a reality orientation group. The staff concerned hoped that her husband and family, and day-centre staff, would be able to carry on the good work at home.

Medical investigations showed that she had a chronic chest condition which caused her to become breathless if she tried to walk more than a few yards.

At the end of the assessment period, lasting some two months, it has been agreed with the family and Amy that she does not need long-term residential care at the moment. After discharge it is planned that Amy will be able to attend a day-care unit three days per week. Although Wesley is going along with this plan he is actually extremely worried that he will not be able to cope. Amy was once so fussy about cleanliness – now she couldn't seem to care less.

ACTIVITY

1 Put yourself in the position of the care worker who is going to prepare Amy for discharge. She is likely to be leaving in two weeks or so.

- Using the 'activities of daily living' model for care described in section 3.11, complete an assessment form for Amy.
- Who would need to know about Amy's discharge? And what would they need to know?
- Where might communications begin to break down?
- What kind of community support do you think she will need? Who will provide this?
- How could her husband be supported?

- How far do you think other members of the family should be involved, and how?

2 Try to summarise Amy's needs on a discharge plan. Whichever format you decide to use:

- include specific goals;
- describe the type of care needed to achieve these goals;
- suggest when and how the goals should be evaluated.

3 When you have completed these tasks, compare your approach with colleagues, and discuss the process with your supervisor.

4 Implementing care

4.1 Caring relationships: *Being aware of yourself*

This section is about how well you know yourself, and your attitudes to old age and older people. Self-awareness can be gained in many ways:

- by observing your own behaviour and reactions in different situations;
- by thinking about your own behaviour and feelings;
- by other people telling you what they think about you.

Why is self-awareness important?

Earlier sections have shown how social attitudes towards older people are often negative. Even within branches of the caring occupations, caring for older clients is often unpopular. But negative attitudes are not only 'out there', they can also be 'in here' – within each of us. Those of us who have committed ourselves to work in this field may find it difficult to accept that our own attitudes may be at fault from time to time. It is all too easy to ignore our own biases and prejudices. Play on the safe side; assume that we all hold *some* negative attitudes – and try to discover what yours are. By questioning ourselves regularly about this, we are less likely to get into a caring rut. Remember that the ultimate aim is to improve client care: our attitudes are an important element in this.

ACTIVITY

This exercise is concerned with self-image or identity. Ask yourself the question, 'Who am I?' Write the answers, each in not more than two or three words. For example:

> I am ... a care worker
> I am ... a husband

and so on. Try to do this exercise at the same time as colleagues. When you have finished, discuss the following points with them.

- How did your answers compare with those of your colleagues?
- How far do you think your answers are a genuine reflection of yourself, and how far do they describe the sort of person you'd like to be?
- What are the implications of this for you in your role as a care worker?

ACTIVITY

Is there a client in your care who reminds you of someone you have known before – perhaps a relative, a friend or another client? If so, how far does your previous relationship affect how you behave towards the present client? Think carefully about this. Do certain characteristics in clients – appearance, manner, tone of voice and so on – trigger particular responses in you? Always try to see clients as they are: don't let yourself be influenced by other relationships.

ACTIVITY

When you look ahead to old age, how does this prospect make you feel?

- Do you think that your own attitudes to old age affect how you care for your clients?
- Are there any differences between what you feel about

old age and how you encourage your clients to feel? If so, why do you think this is? Does it matter?

Make a note of your responses to these questions and discuss them with colleagues.

ACTIVITY

Imagine you have reached the age of 80. Describe how you see:

- yourself;
- your immediate environment;
- your lifestyle.

You might have said, 'I hope I'm like Mrs Beecham when I'm her age!' What is Mrs Beecham like?

If you have painted rather a rosy picture of your own old age, ask yourself how you would cope if you had limited mobility or vision. How well would you manage?

ACTIVITY

You may have noticed that you play different roles when caring for different clients, or for the same client at different times. You could be any one of the following:

- *A stranger* – behaving formally and establishing an initial working relationship. This is always the case when you first meet the client. But it also occurs when caring for clients with very poor memories: for them almost every encounter is a new one.

- *A resource person* – when you give answers to specific questions or provide practical help on the basis of your expertise.

- *A surrogate* – because of the age gap, you may be treated like a substitute grandchild or child, depending on your age. This is perfectly normal – indeed you may

see the client as in some way representing a grandparent-like figure. Problems only arise when your own needs start to push aside those of the client. Older people who have become confused might actually believe that you *are* their husband or wife, brother or sister; but this is a rather different matter, suggesting mental confusion.

Think about whether there are any other roles that you have become aware of in your work. Are you always conscious of the role you are playing? What features in other people do you find influence the kinds of roles you play? Think about age, appearance, tone of voice, ethnic background, social background, gender and sexual orientation – whether someone is gay, lesbian or heterosexual.

ACTIVITY

Relationships with other staff can be as important as those with clients.

- Can you use the suggestions in the previous activity to apply to the roles that you adopt with members of staff?

- Do your attitudes to staff differ from your attitudes to clients? What are these differences?
- How far have you been able to share these feelings with other members of staff?

Reading on . . .

★ *Human Relationship Skills* by Richard Nelson-Jones, published in 1986 by Holt, Rinehart & Winston, is worth reading if you want to explore your relationship skills further.

4.2 Caring relationships: *Communication and its problems*

Successful caring for older people relies heavily on effective communication. But good communication is not easy. Complaints of poor communication are part of everyday life in almost all organisations. Ageing often brings with it a range of very specific communication problems.

Communication is a broad activity and can take many forms. It includes:

- conversations between you and the client;
- giving verbal reports to other members of staff;
- writing care plans.

Face-to-face communication is often divided into two forms: 'verbal' and 'non-verbal':

- *verbal communications* spoken words – questions, statements, explanations, and so on;
- *non-verbal communications (NVC)* smiles, eye contact, nods, posture, appearance, proximity, gestures, and the like.

The question of communication must be considered when planning and implementing care. For example, gestures don't always mean the same in different cultures – in some Asian communities, for instance, shaking the head can mean 'yes', not 'no'.

What is communication?

One way of looking at communication between people is to examine the different stages involved. These stages are:

- *sensation* – being aware of a stimulus;
- *perception* – making sense of these sensations;
- *decision-making* – deciding what to do next;
- *action* – carrying out the decision.

The diagram shows how these stages might work in practice.

Each of the four stages requires specific skills and abilities; and each stage can be influenced by the ageing process and those illnesses that frequently affect older people.

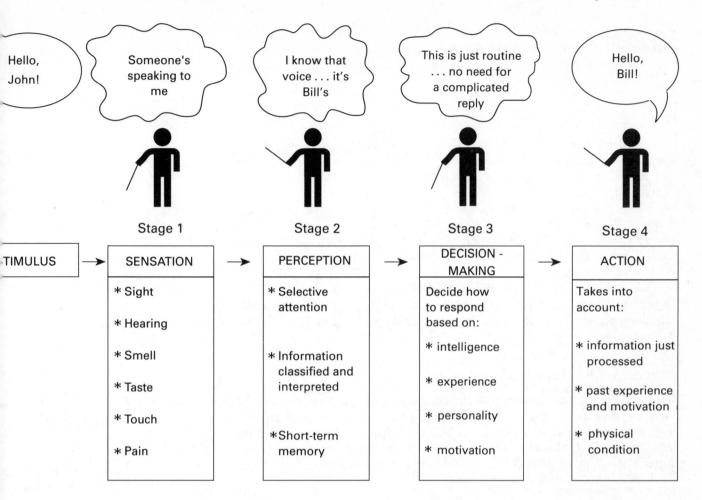

Communication difficulties

Stage 1: Sensation

Ageing causes changes in vision. For instance, the vast majority of older people need spectacles for reading because of increasing difficulty in focusing. While this may be more of an inconvenience than a handicap, serious problems such as cataracts – in which the lens of the eye becomes cloudy – can occur. Worsening eyesight leads to further problems, such as bumping into things, falls and fractures, inability to write letters or watch television, social isolation and disorientation.

Hearing problems are widespread amongst older people. Common changes include difficulty in detecting high frequencies. This reduces the pleasure of listening to music and also makes it more difficult to distinguish between words that sound much the same, especially where there is a lot of background noise. Half-heard conversations can become a source of frustration, even suspicion. Telephone conversations are more awkward, and there can be an apparent decline in intelligence because of the clients' difficulties in registering questions accurately. Deafness is embarrassing to many sufferers and they may try to hide it. As a result, effective treatment might be delayed and social isolation increases.

Taste buds (the sensory organs of taste situated on the tongue) and the olfactory bulbs (the sensory organs of smell located in the nose) work closely together. Notice how food seems less tasty when you have a cold and your nose is blocked. It is usually assumed that ageing decreases the efficiency of these sense organs, but hard evidence is as yet difficult to come by. Older people can be heard to complain that food today is not as tasty as it used to be, although changing horticultural practices as well as declining taste and smell may be to blame.

Stage 2: Perception

Ageing makes it more difficult to both maintain and shift attention. There are many implications here for everyday life. Driving a car, getting used to new environments, taking part in conversations – all will be affected to some degree.

Making sense of our surroundings also depends on our short-term memory. If this begins to fail, information will be lost before it can be properly integrated into our experience and so given meaning. Normal ageing can cause some loss; and brain disorders, such as dementia, may cause severe damage.

In other cases, disorders may lead to clients being unable to understand speech or recognise common objects. Conditions that severely reduce the blood supply to the brain – strokes, for example – can give rise to these problems.

Stage 3: Decision-making

In order to make rational decisions, we need to make the most of our mental faculties, such as intelligence, personality, level of motivation, memory and judgement. Problems with sensation and perception also have an effect on decision-making. The most obvious problems are seen when clients are suffering from progressive conditions that affect the functioning of the mind in all its aspects – senile dementia, for example.

Stage 4: Action

Decisions need to be converted into actions. There are many ways in which this can fail to happen. Sometimes, after a stroke, clients know the words they want to use but can't get the right muscles to work properly. In other cases, clients have a clear idea of the meaning of what they want to say but just can't think of the words to use. It is understandable that many older clients in this position get very frustrated, and they may express this.

Ageing also causes our bodies to be less supple (due, for example, to arthritis). Because of this, non-verbal communications (most noticeably 'body language') may be less effective.

4.3 Caring relationships: *Helping with communication problems*

Keeping in touch with the world forms the basis of our whole existence. Because of this there are few more important or satisfying roles for care workers than to try to reduce the communication problems of their clients. Failure to communicate well is a serious blow to self-esteem. It makes the limitations of old age very obvious. Care workers should do all they can to avoid this consequence.

Effective communicators use a wide range of communication skills:

- they ensure that the environment is suitable for good communication;

- they choose words carefully;
- they use non-verbal methods to enhance what is said.

Communication requires concentration as a listener, for older clients should always be given enough time to absorb what is being said and time to respond.

As a care worker, you should be able to help clients with specific communication problems. In every case, it is vital to cooperate and collaborate with the specialist professional directing the care.

Helping with difficulties in vision

- A well-lit environment is necessary to allow clients to make maximum use of their remaining sight.
- Make sure that the client can see you clearly before speaking, by kneeling down to maintain eye contact, or not standing in front of a window in sunlight, for example. This will improve both verbal and non-verbal communication.
- Always explain what is happening, in language that is simple but not patronising, to prevent any confusion arising.
- Make sure that clients have regular eye checks with a qualified optician.
- Spectacles should be kept clean. Make a point of checking this, especially with clients who have problems in expressing their needs verbally. Ensure spectacles fit properly.
- Signs should be large enough to read easily and lettering should stand out (i.e. there needs to be sufficient contrast between lettering and background). Use lower-case letters, not capitals – these are easier to read because of their more varied and recognisable shapes and patterns.
- Make available large-print books.
- Contact the RNIB Talking Book Service and the National Listening Library, both of which provide taped books; some tapes are available in Welsh, Gujarati, Bengali, Urdu, French and German.
- Magnifiers, some with special stands, can be obtained to make reading or sewing easier.

Helping with difficulties in hearing

- Sit or stand in front of the client, and stay close, so that your lip and facial movements can be easily seen. Keep eye contact and use touch to emphasise points. Wherever possible position yourself so that your face is well lit.
- Be prepared to repeat what you say without getting impatient.
- Don't shout. Apart from anything else, shouting produces distortions in the face that make lip-reading more difficult. Speak firmly, clearly and more slowly than usual.
- Make sure that hearing aids are working effectively and arrange for regular hearing tests.
- Lower the background noise where possible during conversation.
- Use special aids as appropriate, for example 'visual doorbells' (flashing-light doorbells that either switch on all the house lights when there is a caller or operate specific lights only) and visual alarm clocks.
- Special aids are available to assist in listening to television or a hi-fi

system. These allow clients to listen at the volume they need without disturbing others. More and more television programmes have subtitles that can be accessed through teletext.

- Telephones can be adapted to provide a visual display. Alternatively telephones can have built-in adjustable amplifiers. Some hearing aids pick up sound directly from the telephone headset and relay it straight to the listener.

Helping with speech problems

- Don't criticise good attempts at speech, even when many mistakes are made. Relearning the skills of speech will only take place in a supportive and encouraging atmosphere.
- Give clients enough time. On no account should you hurry them.
- Ask questions that provide helpful cues. 'Would you like brown or white bread?' is more useful than 'Which kind of bread would you like?'
- It can be helpful to give the client the first sound of a word.
- Communication charts can be used in severe cases. The speech therapist will advise on the type, for example pictures or words only. Electronic aids may be suggested.
- If speech is found to be almost impossible, continuing to concentrate on it will lead only to very great frustration. With these clients a form of simple sign language may be needed. 'Makaton' is one such language.
- Paper and pen may be helpful and might persuade the client to continue to try to communicate. Alphabet boards could also be tried.
- A healthy mouth aids clear speech. Ensure that dentures fit well and that the client receives regular check-ups from a dentist.
- Older people whose first language is not English need help from care workers or others with knowledge of the clients' language, preferably relatives or friends.

Finding out more . . .

★ More about the Talking Books Library can be found by writing to 12 Lant Street, London SE1 1BR. The Royal National Institute for the Blind (RNIB) can be found at 224 Great Portland Street, London W1N 6AA.

★ Information can also be obtained from the British Association of the Hard of Hearing, 7/11 Armstrong Road, London W3 7JL; the British Deaf Association, 38 Victoria Place, Carlisle, Cumbria CA1 1HU; and the Royal National Institute for the Deaf, 105 Gower Street, London WC1E 6AH. Clients who are both deaf and blind should know about the National Deaf–Blind League, 18 Rainbow Court, Paston Ridings, Peterborough PE4 6UP.

★ ADA (Action for Dysphasic Adults) works for improvements in care for people who have lost some or all of their ability to use speech. They publish a number of *How to Help . . .* booklets designed for dysphasic people and their carers.

ACTIVITY

Choose three clients who experience different communication problems. Review their care and ask yourself these questions:

- What are the causes of each these problems?
- How is the planned care directed towards improving communication?
- Are there ways in which the care plan could be improved?

4.4 Caring relationships: *Communications skills*

This section describes the basic communication skills that you need in order to develop and maintain helping relationships with older clients. Remember that all relationships should be built on a foundation of trust and honesty. Without this, none of these techniques will be of any use whatsoever. Remember also that communication skills have to be moulded into an individual style that suits each care worker and each client. There is no single correct way to do this, but there are ways of refining your skills and of avoiding many of the pitfalls.

Listening

Listening is much more than just hearing. Surprisingly, perhaps, to do it well is much harder than most people think. Listening is an active process requiring conscious effort to pay attention. Good listeners show this in many ways, including eye contact, nodding, keeping an alert posture and by trying to create the right environment. There is little use in setting out to listen attentively while serving lunch. Skilled listeners attend as much to the underlying meaning of what is being said as to the words themselves. This involves being sensitive to the non-verbal aspects of communication:

> 'How are you today, Wes?'
> 'OK, I suppose.'

The meaning of this reply depends on the way it is said and the accompanying actions. It doesn't take too much imagination to think of ways in which the same words could convey a range of emotions from cheeriness through mild irritation to gloomy depression.

Reflecting

A care worker might choose to follow up Wes's reply by saying 'You suppose . . .', using a questioning tone of voice. Repeating the words used by the client is known as *reflection*. In this way you give him the chance to make his meaning clear.

Good communication can only take place when both sides understand what is going on. It is the care worker's responsibility to act as a competent midwife to the client's meanings.

Questioning

We all know how useful questions are for starting up a conversation. However, questions can be quite controlling in that they can encourage or discourage clients to express themselves. *Closed questions* only allow a restricted answer:

> 'What would you like to drink, Mrs Singh?'
> 'Tea, please.'

or:

> 'Mr Reilly, how old are you?'
> 'Eighty-three.'

Obviously these questions produce the kind of response needed at the time.

They get at the information needed. They would be less suitable as a way of starting a longer conversation.

Open questions, on the other hand, are designed to give more chance for expression:

> 'You seem to be looking tired today, Grace. How have you been feeling lately?'
> 'Well, I have been a bit down in the dumps. I haven't seen my granddaughter for a couple of months and I'm rather worried.'

or:

> 'What did you think of the test match, Mr Braithwaite?'
> 'Yes, the West Indies won again, of course, but I could tell you about when they had a *real* team!'

Both examples show how the correct phrasing of a question can encourage a fuller response. The techniques are quite simple but errors are common. Care workers who wonder why they are unsuccessful in getting clients to talk should examine their use of questions. Often the problem lies in using closed questions when the open type is called for.

Summarising

Before moving to a new topic, or ending the conversation altogether, summarise what you understand to be the essential points. Casual conversations do not need to be so formal, of course. But where you have been in serious discussion about a topic of concern to the client it is wise to conclude with a summary.

Using humour

You don't need to be a stand-up comedian to be an effective communicator, but a healthy sense of humour is essential in developing helping relationships. Sensitive use of humour can relieve stress, lighten an otherwise tense atmosphere and bring people closer by sharing a joke or an amusing incident. It is an underestimated skill in caring, probably because it is so elusive. Nevertheless, smiling, humour and laughter are vital ingredients in care – as long as you are laughing with, not at, the client.

Care workers can make creative use of all kinds of humorous opportunities. Jokes can be shared, cartoons enjoyed, comedy films watched. Older people often have clear recollections of the earlier comedians, such as Stan Laurel, Oliver Hardy and Charlie Chaplin. Many of their early black-and-white films have acquired cult status in recent years and are available on video. Why not enjoy them together?

Empathy

Empathy is the ability to see the world from the client's point of view. It is not a distinct skill, like listening, but an ability to bring together a number of skills in such a way that clients feel that you are trying to understand their situations honestly and genuinely. It is quite separate from simply liking or being interested in the client. You must regularly check your interpretation of events with the client:

> 'Now, have I got this right . . .'

and

> 'You seem to be saying . . .'

are two useful ways of starting to do this. Always give the client an easy opportunity to disagree with your interpretation of events, so that you can both get back on to the same wavelength once again.

Pitfalls to avoid

- *Don't be a 'clockwork listener'* – someone who just goes through the motions but whose mind is somewhere else altogether.

- *Don't use unrealistic reassurance*, for example: 'You shouldn't worry, Mrs Salter, everything is going to be all right.' How can you be so sure? What if you are wrong?

- *Don't talk for the client* – the BBC radio programme *Does He Take Sugar?* wasn't called that for nothing! It can be tempting at times to hurry things along a bit, especially when you are busy and the client's speech may be slow or indistinct. But resist the temptation, and stand up for the client's right to express things for herself unless absolutely impossible.

- *Don't hurry important conversations* or start them when you know, or strongly suspect, that you will run out of time. If you are short of time, be honest and say so. Don't let your body language say it for you, for example by fidgeting or looking the other way.

- *Don't give hasty advice* – helping relationships do benefit from sound advice at the right time, but many important problems are solved by the client with the support of an empathic care worker.

- *Don't ask very personal questions* unless you are sure they are necessary and you are in private. Intimate subjects should only be addressed, if at all, in the client's own time and when the relationship has had a chance to develop.

- *Don't assume a client will always know what you mean* – choose your words carefully to suit the person. Some words have changed their meaning – 'gay', for instance – and new words have been introduced, such as 'stereo' and 'feedback'.

Some types of problem will require professional counselling and should not be tackled by care workers who are untrained in these skills. Nevertheless, you should aim to be aware of your own limitations so that you know when to pass the client and his or her problem on to an appropriately qualified person. Always discuss problems of this kind with your supervisor.

ACTIVITY

The best way to learn communication skills is to communicate – under supervision. But the safest way to practise is to begin by role-playing with colleagues. To get the most out of role-play, the ideal is to have one person playing the client, one the care worker, and one or two observers.

Arrange to have half an hour or so in a quiet, undisturbed environment. Try out the skills described in this section by setting up short role-plays – five minutes maximum. Try the following:

- Talking to a rather nervous client who has just started to come to the day centre. You have been asked to get to know her and find out her interests with a view to her joining one of the activity groups.

- Communicating with a client who has a visual prob-

lem. (Simply shut your eyes or smear spectacles with a little flour and water to simulate poor sight.)
- Communicating with a client who has problems in hearing. (Cottonwool should do the trick in this case.)
- Try sitting in a wheelchair, to discover how it feels when the care worker is standing up.

Take turns in being client, care worker and observer. After the role-play, each person should be allowed to say how he or she felt about the experience – care worker first, 'client' second and observers third. Be strict about this sequence.

Role-play can become quite involved and intense when emotional issues are being dealt with. For these exercises, choose unemotive topics so that you can concentrate fully on the skills of communication.

4.5   Caring relationships: *When things go wrong*

Human relationships change constantly. Sometimes they run like a well-oiled machine; at other times, grit gets into the works and progress is less smooth. It is wise to assume that caring relationships will be subject to the same kinds of problems. As a result, even the most dedicated and competent care worker will experience anger, a sense of failure, disappointment, disillusionment and conflict. If you can accept this, you can often avoid or overcome difficulties when they arise.

Acknowledging failures

Failures in relationships are never pleasant; but we can often learn from them. They make us think – about ourselves, about the situation, about how we might do things differently next time. Most important, failure teaches us humility, while at the same time making us more determined.

Disliking a client

There are times when almost every care worker feels anger or dislike towards a particular client. Some staff deny that they ever feel this way, saying that the relationship with the client is a professional one and that therefore liking and disliking are irrelevant. Others blame themselves if they feel negatively towards a client, interpreting it as a failure. But you need to remember that both care workers and clients are human beings. Some aspects of our behaviour will be the results of emotions rather than rational thought. No one is to be blamed when care workers find that they don't get on with particular clients. Again it is an opportunity for learning. By being open with colleagues and discussing your feelings, new approaches to the client may be suggested that might resolve the problem. At the very least colleagues will be aware of the problem and can offer support. Sometimes, where a key-worker system is in operation, it may be helpful to reallocate the client to another care worker, at least for a period.

Dealing with anger and aggression in clients

Serious physical aggression is rarely encountered in the care of older clients. When it does occur, it is usually due to confusion and disorientation and is not generally sustained. A confused client may see a care worker as a threat and this may lead to aggression – most often verbal. Knowledge of the client is the best safeguard in all cases. By having an understanding of how the client reacts, it is often possible to defuse potential aggression. Examples of effective strategies include the tactful use of humour, distraction by changing the topic of conversation, and quietly listening. Section 4.27 provides more guidance on how to manage the problem of aggression.

Perhaps the greatest challenge for care workers is how to deal with the emotions that aggression provokes in themselves. The natural reaction to an aggressive 'attack' is retaliation. One of the values of becoming more self-aware is that it becomes possible to monitor feelings of this kind. Being aware gives us the chance to control our own responses. In this way we can prevent ourselves from responding to the client in a hostile way which would simply make matters worse.

Talking things over with colleagues is essential. Feelings that have had to be controlled still have to be dealt with. Releasing feelings of anger with – not at – other members of staff can avoid a build-up of tension.

Burn-out

People who have worked in caring occupations for some time may start to feel disillusioned and find difficulty keeping their interest in the job. In its severe form this is referred to as *burn-out*.

Signs

Signs of burn-out include:

- fatigue and exhaustion;
- sleep problems;
- less satisfaction from work;
- boredom;
- cynicism and defensiveness;
- irritability;
- loss of effectiveness at work;
- increased alcohol intake.

Causes

Causes of burn-out include:

- abnormally high or prolonged stress levels at work (note: a certain degree of stress usually *improves* performance);
- social isolation;
- poor relationships outside work;
- too few chances to unwind;
- excessively high expectations of self and others;
- lack of adequate support at work – from managers or colleagues.

Prevention

Certain strategies can help to prevent burn-out:

- *Self-care* – don't forget that there is more to life than being a care worker. Make sure that you keep a range of outside interests. Look after yourself by getting adequate exercise and eating sensibly.
- *Ring the changes at work* – discuss with your supervisor how you might change working patterns, try new approaches and take some risks to prevent getting into a rut.
- *Share problems* with your supervisor and colleagues. Don't bottle up worries about work. Make use of opportunities for personal supervision.
- *Have realistic expectations* about your own capabilities. There is no such thing as the perfect care worker!

Supervision

In all the difficult situations described in this section, regular discussions with your supervisor should help to prevent or lessen problems. If supervision is not a part of your usual way of working, discuss with your manager the possibility of introducing it.

ACTIVITY

Notice when you next feel angry with a client. Think about:

- Your specific feelings – what did you feel like? How did you react? How did you *want* to react? Did you control your feelings with difficulty?
- The reasons why you felt this way – what exactly was it about *that* particular client or situation?
- What you learnt from this experience – how might you deal with things differently next time?

4.6 Keeping in touch: *Family and friends*

Throughout our lives we depend on others to meet many of our needs and to give us our sense of identity. For most of us, family and friends are the two pillars that we lean on most for this.

When clients come into care, the continuity of their relationships is threatened. This occurs whether the care is residential, or on a day or domiciliary basis. Although residential care introduces the most obvious barriers, even care in the client's own home can create changed relationships. Relatives and friends may feel, for example, that their role is being interfered with, or they may believe that their caring role has been taken over by the professionals and that they are now expected to limit their involvement. Although all of these feelings can be minimised by properly planned care, they may continue to influence the relationships between clients and their families and friends.

Making family and friends feel welcome

The contacts that occur between clients' visitors and care workers are crucial to the success of care planning. It is not unusual for relatives to feel guilty when a loved one has to accept help from the caring services, especially residential care. This can make positive relations between relatives and care workers more difficult. By being aware of this, care workers can ensure that relatives are involved from the start and are treated with honesty, understanding and kindness.

Most homes operate open visiting arrangements where there are very few limitations on time. It is important for clients and their visitors to be able to meet in private – especially when it is a spouse or partner who is visiting. Physical contact is essential in most loving relationships and does not disappear with the onset of old age. (The topics of sexuality and gender are dealt with in more depth in section 4.9.)

Care workers should help clients to engage in activities with their relatives and friends. For instance, think of the pleasure a client can give and receive through entertaining his great-grandchildren – perhaps by playing games or by offering drinks and biscuits. You should always be on the look-out for new ways of encouraging independent activity for your clients. Unless clients can offer something to relatives and friends, visiting may become merely a matter of duty.

Letter-writing

A good letter is a source of reassurance as well as information. But writing a letter requires physical skills, ideas and motivation. Older clients can have problems with one or more of these. Where ideas and motivation are no difficulty, care workers should be able to help clients as follows:

- *Special writing implements* Easy-to-grip pens or pencils should be obtained for those who can maintain a grip. Special aids are available that enable writing to take place through movements of the arm and shoulder rather than the fingers.
- *Typewriters* Typewriters can be used by some clients who are unable to grip sufficiently.
- *Word-processors* Personal computers with word-processor software are becoming increasingly common. For clients who would not be

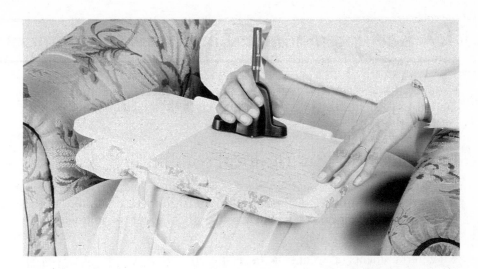

ACTIVITY

1 Select three of your clients. For each, list five occasions where it would be possible to invite family and friends to join in a celebration.

2 Discuss with your supervisor and colleagues how you might try to make the most of each occasion.

ACTIVITY

Some groups of older clients may have particular difficulties keeping in touch. Those who live at a distance from their families and friends are one example. Gay and lesbian clients may find the caring services insensitive to their need to keep in contact with their partners (see section 4.9 for a fuller discussion).

1 Select three clients who have few contacts with family and friends? Why is this?

2 Discuss with your supervisor and colleagues how you could help to improve the situation of each client.

intimidated by this new technology, the word-processor can be a boon and great fun. Such technology has the advantage that it makes very few physical demands. Keyboards are sensitive to the touch, and errors can be corrected before the letter is printed. Only a minimum of controls need be used by clients as care workers can set up the processor ready for use. Confidentiality will have to be considered, however, because the writing will be visible on the computer screen.

- *Care workers as letter-writers* Where physical or psychological reasons prevent clients retaining control over writing, care workers can offer to act as letter-writers. Absolute confidentiality must be maintained when undertaking this role. Great care must also be taken when clients are uncertain of *what* to write. Be careful to ensure that what is written is exactly what the client wants. Always read the letter aloud at intervals to obtain the client's agreement. Remember that writing for a client can take a considerable time. Before promising to help, make sure you have enough time available. Clients may be able and glad to help each other in this way.

With some clients, care workers may need to stimulate interest in writing by giving encouragement and helping clients find topics to write about.

Celebrating special occasions

Regular events, such as birthdays, religious festivals and holidays, offer many opportunities for clients to get together with their family and friends. For some this will mean a chance to have a short break away from the care environment. For others, you will need to help create the opportunity for celebrations to take place within the care home or day centre. There are also many special events that can be exploited in this way, for example the examination successes of grandchildren.

Try to arrange for special occasions to be recorded in some way. Photographs will help to preserve memories of the day. Video recordings may be even better. Suitable equipment can be hired quite easily. Recordings of this kind can also be used to maintain contact with relatives unable to be present on the day. You should help clients to take the initiative on these occasions so that they are not seen as passive recipients of others' favours.

4.7 Keeping in touch: *Local services and networks*

Residential homes and day centres are part of the local community but they can become isolated unless care staff make efforts to create links with their neighbourhood. How can this be achieved?

Information about the local community

You need to have a thorough knowledge of the local area and the available resources. Build up a resource file of relevant information. Make this as wide-ranging as you can, and include information about the following:

- social groups and clubs;
- entertainments (a 'what's on' list is useful);
- tourist information;
- religious services and contacts;
- adult education facilities;
- specific organisations concerned with the elderly;
- bus and train timetables;
- locations of post offices, government departments, banks and building societies . . . .

Think carefully about how you will organise this information for practical use. Some may need to be displayed publicly. In other cases, the information would be better filed with a simple indexing system. Think too about how it might be kept up-to-date. A yellowing poster for last year's pantomime does little to stimulate interest.

The local area and local services

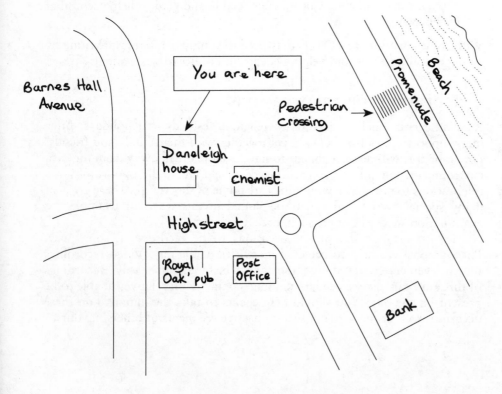

It may be possible to obtain and adapt a commercial map of the area, showing the services that are available. On the other hand, you might prefer to draw your own, and show only what is necessary. Involve your clients as far as possible – ask them for ideas about what they would like to see included, and get them to produce rough sketches. Maps that are to be of everyday practical use to clients could show relative positions not only by distance but also by walking times, bearing in mind the speed of older clients.

Contacts with the community

Try to think creatively to find new ways of making the home or day centre part of local life. All these ideas should be discussed first with clients. The extra stimulation of meeting new people of various ages is usually welcomed by older clients. Some possibilities include:

- *Schools* Many have 'community service' on the timetable and may be interested in the experience offered by a residential home or day centre.
- *Colleges of further education* There is an increasing number of courses in caring. Most include the need for practical experience in a care setting. Contact the college and speak to the lecturer in charge of care courses.
- *Musical and theatre groups* Many are happy to perform on a voluntary basis.
- *Religious organisations* All religions are generally more than willing to be involved in linking with care providers. Many groups arrange regular outings for their members and also visit less mobile clients. Services can also be arranged to take place in the care home.
- *Special-interest groups* There are a large number of organisations catering for specific groups. Examples include ex-forces organisations; professional groups, such as those for retired nurses and teachers; and groups based on ethnic origin. Information about which are available locally is best obtained from local sources, such as the social services department, the Citizens' Advice Bureau and the local library.
- *Local publications* Most towns are also covered by one or more 'citizen's guides' or directories of local services (often published by local newspapers or other commercial concerns). These are full of useful information. If possible, obtain several copies for use by your clients. 'What's on' guides are commonly available, covering details of forthcoming events.
- *Local firms* Some make particular efforts to keep in touch with their past employees.
- *Shops and other commercial businesses* Some outlets are willing to bring their services to customers who can't get out. While this is not desirable if clients can visit the shops with assistance, it can be useful. Visiting hairdressing services are one example.

ACTIVITY

Select four clients. List the various contacts that each person has with the local community. Are there areas that could be developed further? Are there ways in which the experiences of one client could be shared with others?

4.8 Living in groups: *Basic processes*

Most people spend most of their lives in the company of others: family, school, workplace, the community at large. This social group experience shapes our attitudes, guides us in our behaviour and contributes a great deal to our sense of identity and self-worth. You will be able to help clients more effectively if you understand about groups in care settings and how they can influence behaviour.

What is a social group?

Members of a social group share a sense of common identity and tend to behave in fairly predictable patterns. In this sense, a social group is different from a bus queue, where the only common feature is the willingness to stand in the rain for long periods! Groups that arise in care settings vary in their membership and in their duration.

Groups can be formal or informal. Reality-orientation groups are of the formal type. They are set up with a particular purpose in mind – to help keep clients in touch with everyday events – and the roles of participants are relatively clear. Informal groups, on the other hand, occur spontaneously. They develop more haphazardly and are held together by the friendship between members. They frequently cut across the boundaries of formal groups. For example, clients may spend some of their time in formal groups centred on certain activities, such as music or reminiscence. At other times, say when relaxing and watching television, they may have quite different companions.

The value of groups

Groups are of value to their members in the following ways:

- *A sense of belonging* – groups can be supportive and caring, and create a strong sense of security.

- *Learning about self* – clients can learn about themselves from what other group members say.

- *Sharing problems* – many older clients will share similar problems, such as loss of independence, bereavement or health difficulties: recognising that others share many of these is often a very effective way of lessening the burden on each individual.

- *Helping others* – clients may find they can help others in their groups by giving encouragement or practical assistance, such as writing a letter for someone with arthritic hands.

- *Forming and enjoying new friendships.*

Characteristics of groups

A group of older clients will contain an immense amount of life experience. One task of the care worker is to help clients put all that experience to good use. However, being older also means that opinions, biases and prejudices are well established. People may be resistant to any change and this could cause conflict. Because the age range of older clients can be very wide – more than a generation – there will also be many dissimilarities in experience and background. Depending on the catchment area of the care home or day centre, there will be a greater or lesser degree of variation in ethnic background, religion, social class and income. It is no wonder, therefore, that every care group and every client will be unique.

Roles

Members of any group tend to take on certain *roles* within that group. 'Role' refers to the behaviour that is expected of a person in any given position, or *status*. In a group of clients, many of these roles will be informal (as opposed to the staff group, which will be characterised by formal roles: officer-in-charge and cook, for example). However, informal roles are just as significant. Commonly occurring roles are 'joker', 'peacemaker', 'wise person', 'historian' and 'parent'.

The status of clients can change from group to group. Someone who is mildly confused but nevertheless physically able can establish a relatively high status when it comes to helping to prepare for meal-times (laying tables, and so on). However, in a reminiscence group, mental skills will count for more and physical ability less. (See section 4.12 for more on reminiscence.) You should try to identify the strengths of each client and channel them in ways that improve his or her self-esteem.

One of the most obvious roles is that of *leader*. Some clients may appear to be natural leaders. They may take or start discussions, speak for their colleagues, and dominate conversations. However, the loudest leaders are not always the most influential.

Norms

Behaviour rarely if ever occurs in isolation. We are all subject to pressure to conform to either implicit or explicit rules and expectations – or *norms*.

Group norms develop over time. The longer the group has been established, the firmer the expectations of certain patterns of behaviour. Residents who have been together for some years will have created numerous, usually unstated, rules of behaviour. These might affect a wide range of behaviour, for example seating arrangements at meal-times and appropriate ways to dress.

Nothing is completely static, however, and norms are no exception. Should a resident die or leave the group, or should there be mental or physical deterioration in clients, the accepted ways of behaving may well change in order to adapt to the new situation.

Conflict

Groups help people to feel part of a greater whole. However, whenever a group is formed, there is always the potential for conflict as well as cohesion. One of the skills of the care worker in a group setting is to manage conflict creatively and so avoid its damaging consequences. Being sensitive to the state of relationships in the group will enable you to intervene when necessary to defuse a difficult situation. Try to clarify exactly what is going on. Most rows thrive on misunderstanding and muddle. Harmony will never last, however positive a group is most of the time. Conflict is normal, and often useful. It is better for group members to show signs of healthy conflict than for them to be passive and unassertive.

ACTIVITY

1 Make a table similar to that shown here, listing *Groups* you belong to down the side, and the *Value* of these groups across the top. Put +, ++ or +++ in each box depending on how useful each group is. Thus, if you are a member of a sports club and you think that this is very important in forming and enjoying new friendships, put +++ in the appropriate box.

Groups	Values						
	Friendships						
Sports club	+++						

2 Carry out the same exercise for three of the clients in your care. For each person, put +, ++ or +++ according to how far you feel each group encourages him or her to use the experience of being in the group. For example, put ++ in the appropriate box if you think that an informal discussion group is quite good at helping Mr Jones to 'share problems' with other clients and staff.

3 What role does each client play in each group? Are there ways in which you could help clients to learn or adopt new roles?

4 Discuss this exercise with your supervisor and colleagues.

4.9 Living in groups: *Dealing with differences*

Living in groups shows up at once the differences between people. Although there are numerous ways in which clients may differ, sexuality, gender and race are three of the most fundamental.

Sexuality

Sexuality is a pervasive and powerful influence in all our lives. Older clients do not become immune from this influence just because they have passed their sixty-fifth birthdays. Unfortunately, however, the issue of clients and sexuality has long been treated as a taboo subject. Fortunately for the client, a more enlightened approach is emerging.

Sustaining relationships

Some care homes can cater for married couples. Double rooms (and double beds, too) enable intimacy to continue at whatever level the couple wishes. Where couples have been separated by the admission of one or other partner, the situation is more complicated. Much may depend on the mental and physical state of the client, and the attitude of the spouse. Remember that intimacy does not necessarily mean sexual intercourse. A cuddle and a kiss may be just as satisfying and just as necessary for the well-being of the client and spouse. The right to privacy must be ensured, even though this might be difficult in some care homes.

Relationships also develop between clients who meet in residential and day care. While most are friendships of different intensities, some will develop into close, loving relationships. In such cases you should remember that clients in these relationships are entitled to the same privacy and respect that they would enjoy if they were not in care.

Expressing sexuality

In a more general way, you should always try to assess the client's need to express his or her sexuality. Helping clients to look smart and well turned out may be one outcome of this; this is also a way of boosting their self-esteem.

Clients may wish to gain sexual satisfaction through masturbation. Care workers who inadvertently witness this behaviour need to recognise their responsibilities to respond in a discreet and adult manner. If a confused client is masturbating publicly, the care worker should tactfully encourage the client to move to a more appropriate place. Not to do so would jeopardise the dignity of the client. This factor will normally far outweigh any damage done by acting against the immediate wishes of the person concerned.

The needs of those clients who are homosexual (gay or lesbian) should also be recognised. Some care workers may find this an awkward topic to address openly. Others find that the subject clashes with their religious beliefs. Nevertheless, the issue must be considered honestly and frankly if care is not to be discriminatory or oppressive. A few research-based facts on this subject (from Harris 1990) will help:

- most older gays are contented with their sex lives;
- most gays and lesbians prefer partners of their own age;
- older gays have fewer partners than younger gays;
- older gays and lesbians tend to have more friends than their heterosexual counterparts (this may be because they are less able to rely on family support).

It may also be the case that homosexuals are better prepared for ageing because they have had to be more independent, to have better friendship networks, and to learn to deal with stigma and prejudice.

The challenge for care workers is to provide care that is free from bias, to recognise the needs of older clients whose sexual orientation may be different from that of the majority, and to create an atmosphere of tolerance within the care environment.

Gender issues

Mixing the sexes in a care setting should be the usual arrangement: it has many advantages. For most clients this will be the pattern that they have followed for the largest part of their lives. There are exceptions, of course. For example, single men and women who have spent a lifetime in the armed forces and have lived on their own after retirement may not adjust easily to mixing freely with members of the other sex. In these cases you should respect the wishes of the individual as far as possible within the constraints of the care home or day centre. If clients prefer, some activities could be put on for men and women separately.

Irrespective of age, wherever men and women are together, sexuality will influence behaviour in some way or other. The relationship between care worker and client is no exception and, in most circumstances, is a factor that can be put to positive use. For example, many clients will feel good if flattered (for good reason, of course!) by care workers of the opposite sex.

Occasionally, however, distortions may arise in the relationship that can create problems. It is not unknown for clients to accuse care workers of sexual interference, or for clients to make sexual advances towards staff. In all such situations, care workers should ensure that the concern or accusation is raised immediately with the supervisor so that appropriate action can be taken. Nothing is to be gained by turning a blind eye or by laughing it off. Whilst the vast majority of these difficulties will be overcome without serious consequences, they are much harder to put right if the staff involved do not deal with them quickly.

Ethnic issues

Care staff have been heard to comment that ethnic matters are of little importance for them personally because they treat all clients alike, regardless of colour, race or religion. Discrimination, however, is a subtle and insidious process and it is safer to assume that we are all capable of acting in a racist way. By doing so, we keep our minds open to the possibility of prejudice.

The importance of the ethnic background of clients will depend on several factors. The proportions of different groups in the local population is one of these. This will influence the relative numbers in the care setting. The existing community relations between ethnic groups are important too. Your main task is to be aware of your own attitudes towards race and to consider how these may affect everyday work.

Some older clients will be firm in their beliefs, and these beliefs may include prejudice. You will have to judge how realistic it is to confront every expression of prejudice by clients. The mental state of the client will weigh heavily in any decision, as will the likelihood of bringing about change. In contrast to this, however, prejudice on the part of staff members cannot be allowed to go unchallenged. The vast majority of organisations responsible for caring have an explicit equal opportunities policy that incorporates anti-racist and anti-oppressive practice.

ACTIVITY

1 This section and sections 2.2 and 2.3 have looked at how groups can be stereotyped. This exercise asks you to look at your own attitudes to this sensitive problem in greater depth. Do the exercise with colleagues if you can, and discuss your findings with your supervisor. Try to answer the following questions as honestly as you can.

- Are there times when you find yourself responding to older clients in stereotyped ways? Look back at the list of myths in section 2.2 – have you ever shared any of these views?
- If you are female, do you feel that you are or should be better at caring than your male colleagues?
- Do you communicate differently with clients simply according to whether they are male or female? Does it matter anyway? If so, why?
- Are gay and lesbian clients treated differently from their heterosexual colleagues? If so, in what ways?
- Do you find that the sexuality of clients affects how you care for them?

- Do clients from different ethnic origins receive the same care as those from the mainstream culture – white English, in most cases? If so, in what ways? Do the resources available properly meet the needs of each different group? Think about food, hair grooming, language, activities and religious needs, for instance.
- How do you deal with older clients from different ethnic cultures who are isolated? For example, one Sikh and one West Indian amongst twenty white Anglo-Saxons may suffer significant social isolation.

2 If you have discovered that you sometimes respond to clients as stereotypes, what can you do to change this? Is it possible, and do you want to?

3 As a member of a care team, what can you do to ensure that all clients receive the same standards of care regardless of their background, ethnic origin, colour or other physical characteristics, religion, gender or sexuality?

4.10 Keeping and developing interests: *Activities*

Being alive is about being active. We need to remain active throughout life in order to exercise the body and to stimulate the mind. Work and play are both important aspects of being active and creative. Although ageing brings about changes in our responsibilities and capabilities, as a care worker you should pay close attention to the occupational, leisure and recreational needs of your clients.

Assessment

As part of the assessment, try to find answers to the following questions:

- *What are the client's current activities and interests?* As sections 3.6 and 3.16 show, one of the harmful effects of entering residential care is that it can mean doing less. It follows that what clients do now may not be an accurate measure of what they are *capable* of doing.

- *What were the client's past interests and activities?* The fact that past activities are not being followed now does not mean that clients have lost interest in them. It could be that they are no longer physically able to pursue them. Sport is an obvious example: the keen cricketer at 20 is likely to be an interested follower of the test match results at 80. Alternative activities such as watching (live or on television), reading or discussing can be acceptable substitutes – never as good as the real thing, of course, but absorbing all the same.

- *What are the client's current needs and abilities?* Once you have answered the first two questions, you might find that there are a variety of needs, not currently being met, that could be tackled with appropriate activities, either old or new.

Taking risks

Every activity entails some degree of risk. When clients are older they need to give a little more thought to the suitability of activities. Hang-gliding may be only for the few but it does not follow that everyone wants an unremitting diet of board games.

Caution can be taken much too far. Possible risks must be carefully balanced against the potential benefits to the clients of undertaking an activity. And it should be recognised that individual clients – provided that they are capable of rational decision-making – have the *right* to expose themselves to a degree of risk in just the same way as they would were they not receiving care. Attempts to place restrictions on older clients are often done simply to relieve the anxieties of the staff.

Kinds of activities

What follows is not a comprehensive list of activities but some suggestions intended to stimulate your ideas for caring in a more creative way. Imaginative caring must include giving the clients plenty of chances to show what they are capable of doing. Concentrate on activities that clients find enjoyable and that minimise their weaknesses and limitations.

Being a resource

Try not to let clients feel that they are always on the receiving end. Older people have something to offer. Experiences and memories can be put to good use for the benefit of others. Schoolchildren or college students can have the past brought to life for them by talking to people who have experienced it: older clients can be unique sources of oral history. Learning about the way that people lived thirty, forty and fifty years ago is a means of putting the present into perspective.

Many older clients wish to pass on their cultural traditions. Young people can be involved in various ways, from asking questions to helping to collect pictures and other objects that represent aspects of the culture. These materials can then be used later for other clients or young people.

Clients might want to get involved in local or national charity events. Collecting used stamps, knitting or sewing, or raising plants are just some of the possibilities for fund-raising. If organised on a group basis, even those clients with serious physical or mental disabilities can play a role.

Reading

This is perhaps the most common activity of all, yet one that can so easily be lost to older clients, through either visual problems or other physical or mental limitations. Reading can be converted into a social activity by introducing poetry or play reading.

Music

Some clients will have a talent for music and be able to play a musical instrument. Wherever possible, arrangements should be made to allow this to continue. Recent technology has helped considerably. Although it may be impossible to acquire a full-size piano, small electronic keyboards can give a good deal of pleasure. For those clients with arthritic fingers, this may be the only realistic option. Some models will also allow the player to listen through headphones and so play without disturbing others.

Headphones can also be used when listening to recorded music; the listener can be in raptures while others continue their conversations or watch television in peace. Personal stereos are also a possibility and are relatively cheap. The controls are rather fiddly, however, so these will not be suitable for everyone.

The choice of music needs some thought. In this country, present-day pop music began in the 1950s and those who are 80 now were only in their forties then. As time goes by we continually need to make these kinds of mental adjustments so that we are prepared for the client who prefers Elvis Presley and the Beatles to songs from the Second World War. Other clients may be interested mainly in classical music.

Although music can be a great boon, it can also be seriously abused in care settings. Music is there for the clients. Staff who, regardless of the wishes of the clients, tune in the radio to a pop music station and leave it there indefinitely could justifiably be accused of neglect.

Television

Television has been much maligned in the past because of the potential for abuse through indiscriminate use. Ask the clients to discuss and decide what they want to see. If a video recorder is available more clients will be able to see what they wish.

Art and craft

This can range from an appreciation of fine art – visits to local art galleries, or specialist books from the library – to skills that clients wish to continue or new ones that they would like to acquire. The potential is vast. Remember, you don't have to have all the skills yourself. Most staff can contribute one or two skills and it is important that these are pooled for the benefit of clients. Volunteers can also help; it's a good idea to investigate local clubs and organisations that might be interested.

Sports and games

There are activities to suit all interests and abilities. For example:

- indoor bowls (you'll need a reasonable stretch of carpet);
- table games, including draughts, chess and card games;
- group games, such as quizzes or bingo.

Gardening

Most day centres and care homes have areas of garden. If not, there are more than enough indoor opportunities for the keenest gardener. The constant temperatures normally available are ideal for trying out more exotic indoor plants, such as aubergines and peppers (capsicums): if successful, these can also be used to widen the menu. There are many special aids now available to help older clients continue their hobby both indoors and out. The organisations listed at the end of this section will be able to provide further information and ideas. Plant and seed catalogues can be obtained by referring to the small advertisements in national papers. Visits to garden centres can provide valuable ideas as well as goods to buy.

Pets

Pets are becoming more common in care settings. For many older clients, a relationship with a pet dog or cat means a great deal – especially for those who have lived, or who live, alone. Not all residential homes or day centres will welcome pets. The demands of hygiene and the extra work can be a disincentive. Indoors, cagebirds and aquariums are usually little bother. And, if there is room outside and the location is suitable, ducks, chickens, pigeons or a goat can be stimulating – and sometimes productive – companions.

Social events

There are many possibilities:

- Games evenings, perhaps trying to create a 'pub' atmosphere: it's worth contacting a local brewery or pub to see whether they will help out with materials (for example, beer mats and advertising posters) to create atmosphere.

- An Afro-Caribbean or Chinese day or evening, with appropriate foods, drinks and displays. Local associations may be able to help with advice and equipment. These might be linked to particular religious or cultural celebrations.
- The formality of a dinner-dance also appeals to some older clients. It is often surprising how many past skills – such as dancing – return when given the chance.

Finding out more . . .

★ Horticultural Therapy, Goulds Ground, Vallis Way, Frome, Somerset BA11 3DW (0373 64782).

★ Gardening Trust, Hayes Farm House, Peasmarsh, Sussex TN31 6XR.

★ For a recent discussion on 'risk-taking, safety and older people', see *Living Dangerously* by Deirdre Wynne-Harley, published in 1991 by the Centre for Policy on Ageing (071–253 1787).

ACTIVITY

The choice of activities can be very confusing. One way through the maze, however, is to find a way of describing activities that relates them to the needs of the clients. The diagram shows one way of doing this. Enter different activities in the left-hand column. Then add the various requirements: an example is given. Remember that every requirement or demand is also a potential benefit to the client.

Vary the approach to suit different circumstances. The headings could be changed, for instance. What matters is the thought that goes into analysing the various activities and how they might be of value to clients. Try this approach out in your own care setting and discuss your ideas with colleagues.

ACTIVITY	DEMANDS			
	PHYSICAL	PSYCHOLOGICAL	SOCIAL	RESOURCES
Sowing seeds	Read instructions Open packet Handle seeds Write label	Limited concentration	Minimal – can be done individually or in a group	Seeds Seed trays Compost Labels 'Dirty' environment
Crossword puzzle				
Writing letters				

4.11   Keeping and developing interests: *Getting out and about*

Almost everyone appreciates having a break from time to time. Trips, outings and holidays are usually high spots in the year for most clients, particularly those in residential care. Some clients have relatives or friends who are willing and able to arrange for breaks. But many are not so fortunate.

As with most activities, careful planning will lead to the best results. Although a day trip is very different from a week's holiday, they share certain features as far as planning is concerned.

Where to go

The destination will be determined by factors such as these:

- the wishes of the clients;
- the number of clients wanting to go and the number of staff available;
- the cost;
- the availability of suitable accommodation – bearing in mind access to buildings, for example:
- the time available;
- the distance and the travelling time;
- the availability of transport.

Where possible care workers should first take a good look at the place to be visited. You can then check on access for wheelchairs, locate toilets, find suitable activities, and generally reduce your uncertainties. Medical facilities in the area should be assessed, too. It is better to be prepared. If an advance visit is not possible, obtain as much information as you can before making firm plans, and certainly before parting with any cash. Most travel firms and tourist organisations are willing to pass on their views and advice. Local tourist boards usually have an impressive range of leaflets covering everything from places to stay to what's on throughout the year.

Overseas holidays can be particularly suited to the older person, especially if the opportunity is taken to get away off-season when prices are lower and the resorts not so crowded. Clients with chest or joint disorders will usually benefit from a warmer climate.

A number of older clients dislike going away: they fear illness and accident. Their wishes must be respected in this. Nevertheless, always give all clients the fullest possible information about what is involved so that they can make an informed decision.

Before

This is the best part for many people: the anticipation of pleasure to come. Most older people will have had considerable experience in this, having arranged things either for themselves or for their families. For them it will be a case of rekindling old skills. Encourage your clients to obtain books, leaflets and photos connected with the area to be visited so that they can begin to learn something of where they are going. Formal or informal discussions can be arranged to talk over aspects of the trip. Try to ensure that all clients have a say and feel involved.

It is essential for staff to plan the event in as much detail as possible. Crucial aspects include the ratio of clients to care workers. This will depend upon how independent the clients are, both physically and mentally. There should always be enough staff to cope with an emergency without jeopardising the safety of the group as a whole. The overall size of the group should be consistent with the objectives and type of outing. Too large a group will sometimes make clients feel conspicuous. Staff should be willing participants. For a holiday in particular there is nothing worse than having a reluctant member of the party.

During

Points to bear in mind while you are out and about are these:

- On holiday, continue to plan as a group so that clients stay involved and each day has a fresh focus. Find time to relax in the evenings. Review the day's activities and discuss what the next day might hold.
- Try to arrange a balance of activities that reflects the interests of all the clients, not just the dominant few.
- Make sure that someone is keeping a diary of places visited, people met and so on.
- Encourage clients to take photographs. You might think of running an informal competition for the best or the funniest.
- Pace activities so that energies don't get burnt up too soon. Allow for adequate rest breaks in the course of the day.
- Don't do everything as a group. Try to give clients the chance to follow their own individual interests from time to time.
- If cost is a major concern, remember the concessions that are normally available to the older person. Even if these are not advertised openly, always ask, but discreetly.
- Keep some of the free souvenirs of the outing, for example tickets, serviettes and leaflets. They are a concrete reminder of what took place.

After

A day out should last much longer than that in the minds of the clients and staff. And the 'before – during – after' of a two-week holiday will stretch over several months if planned with care. There are many ways in which you can help the images, impressions and memories to last:

- Clients can make photographs into a visual diary of the occasion and the album can be kept available for all to see. Enlargements can be framed and hung in the home or unit. Copies of photos can be made for individual clients.
- Relatives, friends and other care colleagues can be invited to hear about the event. Illustrate what is said with mounted photographs or slides.
- You can make a scrapbook using the bits and pieces collected.
- You can use the occasion in reminiscence and reality-orientation groups.

ACTIVITY

Investigate the opportunities for days out and holidays for your clients. Many travel companies are now targeting their marketing at the older age groups and some are becoming more sensitive to their needs. Build up a resource file of addresses and brochures. How far does what is available match the needs of your clients? Ask clients what they think about this.

Finding out more . . .

★ The Holiday Care Service, 2 Old Bank Chambers, Station Road, Horley, Surrey RH6 9HW (0293 774535) is a registered charity which provides free information and advice on holidays for people with a wide range of special needs. They have over two hundred leaflets on all kinds of topics.

★ Saga Holidays has had nearly forty years of experience of specialising in holidays for people over 60, both in the UK and abroad. They sponsored the publication in 1990 of a Holiday Care Service/ English Tourist Board booklet, *Tourism for All: providing accessible accommodation*. Brochures can be obtained from local travel agents or Saga Holidays Limited, The Saga Building, Middelburg Square, Folkestone, Kent CT20 1AZ (0800 300 500/600).

★ Airtours ('Golden Years Holidays') and Thomson ('Young at Heart') are two companies that have also produced special brochures for the over-55s. These brochures can be obtained from local travel agents.

4.12 Keeping and developing interests: *Reminiscing*

For older people the past often seems to be more vivid than the present. Perhaps this should not be surprising because life before 60 or 65 is often packed full with significant, sometimes dramatic, changes in responsibilities, relationships and financial status. Experience may never be quite as intense again. A further reason for this concentration on earlier years is the knowledge that life does not go on for ever. Older clients often start to review their lives – to try to put past experience into perspective in some way. The need to pay particular attention to the past is therefore a perfectly rational one for the older person. However, care workers should encourage clients to guard against 'living in the past', because positive aspects of the present will become harder to accept.

Reminiscence as a therapy

Reminiscence is structured through a series of activities that have goals and can be used as part of a client's care plan. It is usually carried out in small groups so that there will be plenty of opportunities for discussion between group members. Sessions should not be too long, but the precise length is best decided by the activity and the attention span of the clients – 15–30 minutes is adequate to begin with. Topics for reminiscence are almost limitless and they will change as the client group changes. Here are a few examples:

- lifestyles, and variations in different parts of the country;
- work experiences;
- key events, such as wartime experiences;
- personal life stages, such as school, marriage or having children.

A wide range of resources can be used to bring the topics to life. For example:

- photographs;
- tape recordings – audio or videotape;
- objects of the period, such as household items, clothes and wartime equipment: visits to museums and exhibitions can be arranged;
- food and drink;
- smells – perfumes, flower scents;

- visits – trips to places that have strong associations with the past can be a powerful stimulus to the recall of previous experience: however, they can also be deeply disturbing because emotions may be relived.

Commercial companies can supply ready-made packs of reminiscence materials but much of what might be needed can be home-made. Relatives and friends of both clients and staff will often come up with useful items. To find materials relevant to clients from different ethnic origins, seek advice from local social services departments, and local and national organisations concerned with older people. The more thorough the assessment of the client in the first place, the easier it should be to select appropriate resources.

Reactions to reminiscence

Care workers should never begin reminiscence activities without first considering how clients might respond to the emotions that personal memories can provoke. What reactions can be anticipated?

- *joy* – the pleasure of familiarity;
- *curiosity* – the effort to fill in the details from the past;
- *humour* – much of the past can seem quaint and old-fashioned;
- *surprise* – perhaps in response to the changes that have occurred over the years;
- *interaction and discussion* – as clients recognise what they have in common;
- *strengthened sense of identity and self-worth* – reminiscence emphasises the clients' strengths, in this case the ability to recall the past;
- *sadness and tears* – not all memories can be happy ones.

Reminiscence may occasionally bring out in clients deeper emotions, such as grief or remorse. These may be linked to specific memories that have been triggered but might be part of a more general response to growing older. At times the richness of the past is compared unfavourably with the apparent poverty of the present and future.

Don't be surprised by what may seem negative reactions. They are an inevitable part of the integration of the past and the present that each one of us has to attempt. By sensitive and active listening, you can encourage constructive recall and group discussion. A wary eye should be kept on the possibility of clients expressing highly charged emotions. If this occurs, discuss the circumstances with your supervisor.

Reading on . . .

★ A specialist magazine is available – *Reminiscence* – which is the magazine of the Reminiscence Network. This has been established by Help the Aged to promote good practice. The magazine is lively and varied and is essential reading for any care worker in this field. The multicultural perspective is well represented.

★ Catalogues that include reminiscence materials can be obtained from Nottingham Rehab, Ludlow Hill Road, West Bridgford, Nottingham NG2 6HD (0602 452345) and Winslow Press, Telford Road, Bicester, Oxfordshire OX6 0TS (0869 244644).

MEMBA WEN
(REMEMBER WHEN)
by Ed (Bunny) Panting

Why ole pipple memba de pass dem say
Da becaas fucha dem no get
but yu memba wen Agaas mont
Crab duz de run?
Now calenda lass, da any mont
Dat da dat.

Memba wen ina January
Naat wind duz blow fu whole week
Now if'e blow bout 2 or 3 days
De pipple safe haaba dem seek.

Memba wen Satideh used to be bading day?
Wata mi scase – dat da true
but yu set down yu bowl
Get bucket and blue soap – wash good
De whole week yu smell new.

Memba wen loose plantin
Out da Court House Warf
Yu cud pick dem up – dat da free
If yu inten fu buy –
Den da one whole bunch
and dat de bunch yu need help fu ker.

Memba wen rejeck cucnat
from Cap'n Foot place
Used to sell one cent fu one?
Three cents conch
One cent okra, and one cent coco
gimme dinna plus frittas from de pan.

Memba wen 10th Septemba mi mean straw hat
Wid red white and blue ban
Sal'physic pan yu foot
School rosette pan yu shut and yu flag
fu yu wave ina yu han?

Memba wen LEC ban
di lead Catholic School
Wid Imperial and Colonial behin?
St. John's, St. Mary's
Wesley School and Miss Rocke
Ebeneza and Amy in line?

Baptis, Miss Mehia, Vernon and Robateau
All in di great big parade
Marching up to di Barracks
Fi some games and some fun
Di bag a cake and yu lemanade.

I no kay we dem se
Fu me memry still good
I memba wen an I know dat yu could.

They say old people remember the past
Because they have no future
But you remember when August was the month
When the crabs did their run?
Now it seems the calendar is lost
And they run in any month.

Do you remember when in January
The North wind would blow for a whole week?
Now if it blows for 2 or 3 days
The people seek safe harbour.

Do you remember when Saturday was bathing day?
Water might have been scarce, that's true,
But you set down your bowl,
Got your bucket and blue soap,
Washed well
And you smelled good for the whole week.

Do you remember when loose plantains
Would be lying around at Court House Wharf?
You could pick them up – they were free
If you were buying –
Then there were whole bunches
And you needed help to carry them away.

Do you remember when the reject coconuts
From Captain Foot's Place
Used to sell for one cent each?
A conch for three cents
Okra for one cent, coco for one
Give me dinner with fritters from the pan.

Do you remember when 10th September was the day
For wearing your smart straw hat,
Trimmed with a red and white ribbon
Sal'physic on your feet,
Your school rosette on your shirt and your flag
To wave in your hand?

Do you remember when the LEC band
Led the Catholic School
With the Imperial and Colonial behind?
With St. John's, St Mary's,
Wesley School and Miss Rocke
Ebeneza and the Army following behind?

Baptis, Miss Mehia, Vernon and Robateau
All in this great big parade
Marching up to the barracks
For some games and some fun
A bag of cakes and some lemonade.

I don't care what people say,
My memory is still good
I remember when, and I know that you could.

This poem was the winning entry in the older people's section of a Reminiscence Competition organised by HelpAge Belize, a national voluntary organisation working with older people. The translation and the original appear courtesy of HelpAge International.

4.13   Learning for life: *Reality orientation*

What is reality orientation?

Reality orientation (RO) is a therapy designed to reduce disorientation and confusion amongst older clients and so improve their quality of life.

RO was first used in the late 1950s in the USA. Since then, it has been widely used in the UK in a variety of care settings, from day units to hospital wards. The same principles can also be used in the client's own home by visiting care workers. In most cases, you will be taking part in RO alongside a professionally qualified colleague – an occupational therapist or a social worker, for example.

Who needs RO?

One of the most serious disadvantages of being in residential care is that it is all too easy to lose contact with the outside world. This can happen to anyone – young or old – under certain conditions. But with increasing age, it is often more difficult to overcome the most damaging effects of the process of institutionalisation. As earlier sections have shown, social isolation and sadness are not uncommon in old age. These make it even harder to keep in touch with events in the outside world.

In the case of some older clients, the grip on external reality is severely weakened by organic brain changes – such as Alzheimer's disease – which interfere with memory and the ability to think clearly.

Potentially, then, there is a double problem for care workers. First, how should you organise care so that clients retain contact with the day-to-day occurrences that most of us take for granted – news about our families, neighbourhood and friends, domestic and world news, or sports events? Secondly, how do you offset the effects of failing memory and other psychological problems, for example poor concentration and disorientation? The solution to these problems starts by creating a physical and social environment enabling clients to maintain dignity and autonomy through maximum independence.

RO – the principles

Reality orientation is based on five important principles:

- *Re-learning* of information that is needed to keep in touch with the external world – the time of day and the date, and names of places, people and things, for example.
- *Re-stimulation* of the various senses by deliberately stimulating the full range – touch, smell and taste, as well as sound and sight.
- *Re-socialisation* through group activities which encourage the sharing of experiences and general discussion.
- *Re-motivation* by creating new interests and finding a new purpose.
- *Reminiscence* about important events in the client's past experience. (This is covered in section 4.12.)

The practice of RO

There are two main forms of reality orientation:

- informal (or 24-hour) RO;
- formal (or classroom) RO.

Informal reality orientation

The aim here is for care workers to carry out the principles of RO at all times. In this way the client will be able to keep a firmer grasp on reality. Every conversation with a client is used as an opportunity to remind the person of what is going on, to stimulate interest and to encourage re-learning. An example will help to make this clear.

> *Care worker:* 'Hello, Mr Faiz. It's half-past six now and dinner is ready.'
> *Mr Faiz:* 'Is it that late already?'
> *Care worker:* 'We've got chicken curry tonight. Shall we go to the dining room and get ready? It's been a very stormy day, hasn't it? Did you hear the rain on the windows?'

- 'Hello, Mr Faiz' identifies the client clearly and respectfully: a reminder of who he is.
- 'It's half-past six now' reminds him of the time of day.
- 'We've got chicken curry' encourages him to anticipate the meal.
- 'Shall we go to the dining room . . . ?' is an invitation which helps the client to get a sense of his immediate environment.
- 'a very stormy day . . . did you hear the rain on the windows?' encourages him to remember very recent events and to bring into play a range of senses; in this case hearing in particular is emphasised.

Each statement should be accompanied by helpful body language, such as indicating the dining room and windows. Do this discreetly, however, to avoid being patronising. When you care for someone whose memory is failing, and who is losing contact with immediate reality, try to speak with interest and freshness. For clients with a very poor recent memory, every encounter with a care worker will feel like the beginning of a new relationship. This can be threatening for the clients, so try to sound as if you know them well.

Such 24-hour reality orientation needs the right environment. The aim is to provide an environment that is as clear as possible to the clients by the effective use of signs that help clients keep in touch with everyday reality. There are many specialist aids for this, but home-made ones may be perfectly adequate and have the advantage that they can be changed more often. Commonly used aids are:

- Large-print reality-orientation boards that include information such as:
  - the name of the establishment;
  - the day and date;
  - the month and year;
  - the season;
  - the weather.
  Some boards use pictures to enhance the words. All allow the information to be updated daily.
- Large clocks.
- Location signs, using words or pictures, or both.

None of these aids can substitute for properly structured conversations with clients, but they are helpful in reinforcing what is said by care workers.

Formal reality orientation

This is a more specialised approach, normally conducted by qualified professional therapists. (Nevertheless, care workers may be expected to use informal RO outside the formal sessions.) Small groups of clients meet regularly with the therapist for periods of 20–30 minutes. The demands made on clients depend on just how confused and disorientated they are. For clients who are suffering from severe dementia, it may only be possible to concentrate on basic information, such as name, date and place. More can be expected of the less confused clients. In these cases, topics will be selected that are thought to be relevant and interesting to the group. Examples might be:

- a current event from the newspaper;
- birthdays;
- the weather;
- the season.

Maximum use should be made of a wide range of aids that stimulate several senses. For example, in a session on 'spring' the therapist might introduce film showing new-born lambs or bring in bulbs that are beginning to come into bloom. The bulbs could be passed around the group. With these experiences as starting points, conversation is built up about the topic.

ACTIVITY

1 For a fresh view of your own work setting, try inviting in an outsider. There is an ethical issue here, of course: to ensure that a visitor doesn't become an intruder, you must get the agreement of your supervisor before starting.

With the support of your supervisor, arrange for someone to visit your establishment who has never been there before. You might choose a care assistant from another home, or a person from a quite different area of work. In some ways, a person unconnected with the caring occupations will be more useful because he or she will bring fewer preconceptions.

Ask your visitor to imagine that she has recently been admitted to the home. Then request her to record her impressions of the general environment – how easy it is to find her way around, to find the toilets, telephone, office and so on. You could provide a checklist or leave it to the person concerned.

2 Another way of approaching this would be to design a questionnaire that could be given to relatives or other visitors to the unit. Again, ask them to comment on the environment, its layout and signposting.

3 At the end of the activity, discuss your findings with your supervisor and colleagues.

Reading on . . .

★ You can find out more about this topic in *Reality Orientation: principles and practice* (1982) by Lorna Rimmer. It is published by Winslow Press.

4.14 Learning for life: *Lifelong education*

Much of this book is concerned with education in its broadest sense. Reminiscence, reality orientation, interests and activities all draw on the ability of the clients to learn. This section, however, concentrates on how older clients can take advantage of the more formal aspects of education. In this context, an older person should have the same range of choices as any other adult in the community. An older person who is receiving care of whatever kind should not be disadvantaged in any way because of that fact.

Having said that, it is disappointing to have to record that older people have generally received a raw deal in educational terms. Not all the blame can be put at the door of government for providing insufficient resources, inadequate though these have been. Many people – old and young – have not been raised to expect much from the educational system and so do not always see its relevance in adult life. As with many other parts of our lives, attitudes developed in the early years have a habit of lingering. So, as well as trying to make available the best opportunities for older clients, care workers may need to try to deal with negative attitudes towards education in general.

The goals of education

The goals of education change throughout life. Two phases affect the older person. These are:

- *Early old age* At this time, individuals disengage from the well-established patterns of work, with their controls and time constraints, and also from the need to take complete responsibility for their families. Having more time on their hands allows older people to re-engage in new activities and interests. These can be quite different from their earlier interests. For some, this new situation may give greater freedom to choose a different lifestyle.

- *Later old age* As physical problems increase in frequency, so educational involvement may seem more appealing as a means of preserving personal independence. The body may become restricted by disability or disease, but this need not apply to the mind as well.

There are a number of advantages in making maximum use of education in the care of older people. As a care worker, you should certainly be seeking out ways of enabling clients to remain as independent as possible. Because, for many clients, the mind preserves its freedom longer than the body; education can be an attractive way of helping clients to maintain dignity and self-respect.

Educational organisations

There are many educational organisations that can help older clients. They include those mentioned below.

The University of the Third Age (U3A)

This is a very special organisation because it is run *for* older people *by* older people. It too emphasises the scope for personal fulfilment in old age. Launched in France in 1972, the U3A is an international movement designed to promote education for the older person. It has expanded rapidly and now there are U3As in a great many countries. There are national variations in how they are organised. Some are linked to traditional universities. In other cases, groups are based on the principle of self-help: this is the situation in the UK. Individuals share their learning, so that the person who is a learner today may well be a teacher tomorrow. This is true to the broadest concept of a university, where everyone is offered the chance to add to their stock of knowledge and skills. Learning for its own sake is the main educational aim.

There are opportunities for residential home, day centre and domiciliary care workers to take advantage of the benefits of U3As and similar groups. In addition to encouraging individual clients to involve themselves, some care providers have offered the use of accommodation for U3A meetings. What better way to bring facilities into the reach of clients?

From a leaflet produced by the U3A National Office:

Q. WHAT IS IT?   **A.** An organisation for providing all kinds of educational, creative and leisure activities for anyone not in full-time, paid work.

Q. WHO CAN JOIN?   **A.** Retired people of all ages. No academic or other qualifications are needed [and none are given].

Q. WHO RUNS IT?   **A.** U3A members organise their own activities and offer their own skills, knowledge and experience to their fellow members.

Q. WHERE DOES IT EXIST?   **A.** There are currently more than 160 U3As throughout the UK with some 20 000 enthusiastic individual members. More are starting all the time.

Adult education centres

These organise a wide range of educational programmes, including leisure activities – yoga, art appreciation and cookery, for example – and more formal courses leading to examinations and qualifications.

The Open University

This offers degree or shorter courses made up of study materials, tutorials, assignments and broadcasts. Tutorials are usually given in local centres but tutors can visit students in cases of need.

Universities, polytechnics and colleges

Many of these provide courses for specific groups, including older people. There is no age limit and, in some cases, it may be possible for lecturers to visit care homes to run a course or a day workshop on a topic of interest. Fees will be charged but often at a reduced rate for retired people. Contact the Continuing Education Departments in your local institutions.

Workers' Educational Association

Local centres run courses like those of the universities, polytechnics and colleges.

The National Extension College

This provides distance-learning (correspondence) courses in academic and leisure subjects. They are studied at home at the student's own pace.

ACTIVITY

Try to find out what educational opportunities exist in your area for the older client. Make contact with the following:

- adult education centres;
- a further education college;
- a polytechnic or university;
- the Workers' Educational Association.

Talk to the lecturers responsible for continuing or adult education and ask how they help the older person. Are tutors encouraged to open their courses to all ages? Is there adequate access for people with limited mobility? Do they operate courses on a distance-learning basis, whereby attendance is kept to a minimum and the student does most of the learning at home using books and tapes? Would they be able to provide educational opportunities for older clients receiving care?

Obtain the prospectuses from your local educational institutions. Do they make any reference to the older student?

Reading on . . .

★ For those interested in learning more about the older learner, two recommended books are: *Age is Opportunity: education and older people* by Eric Midwinter, published in 1982 by the Centre for Policy on Ageing, and *Older Learners: the challenge to adult education* edited by Susanna Johnston and Chris Phillipson, published in 1983 by Bedford Square Press (for Help the Aged's Education Department).

★ You can obtain further information from the following: the Third Age Trust/National U3A Office, 1 Stockwell Green, London SW9 9JF (071–737 2541); the Open University, Walton Hall, Milton Keynes MK7 6AA (0908 653231); and the National Extension College, 18 Brooklands Avenue, Cambridge CB2 2HN (0223 316644).

4.15 Meeting physical health-care needs: *Maintaining continence*

By the time we reach the age of five years or so, most of us have managed to gain control over our bladder and bowels. Because these functions are normally achieved in childhood, any return to an uncontrolled state – *incontinence* – is experienced as particularly humiliating and embarrassing. Unfortunately, incontinence is a taboo subject. This makes open discussion more difficult than it should be. By drawing on your practical experience of the problem as a care worker, you can try to change attitudes towards this distressing condition.

For a number of physical reasons, older people are especially at risk of developing incontinence.

Causes of incontinence of urine

Damage to the nervous system

Senile dementia can cause damage to the centre in the brain that controls the emptying of the bladder. The person feels the urge to go to the toilet but finds it increasingly difficult to resist this urge – incontinence is often the result.

Damage to the muscles supporting the bladder

This is a common reason for incontinence in women. Muscles can be weakened by childbirth, obesity and changes related to ageing. Any extra pressure (coughing, sneezing, moving or lifting, for example) will cause so-called *stress incontinence*.

Enlarged prostate gland

In men there is a gland (the prostate gland) that surrounds the urethra just below the bladder. The urethra is the tube that carries urine from the bladder, through the penis and so to the outside. The prostate gland increases in size with age and puts pressure on the urethra, so making it more difficult to pass urine. In some older men there is an almost complete blockage which causes the bladder to become filled with urine. This then acts like a full tank in a domestic plumbing system – extra urine produced by the kidney overflows. The problem for the client is that urine is then lost in small amounts almost continuously, and it is virtually impossible to remain dry.

Other factors

Mobility

Being less agile, many older people will find it impossible to reach the toilet in time. There may also be problems with removing clothing in preparation to pass urine.

Environment

The distance to the toilet may be too great. Access to the toilet may be awkward, for example doors may be hard to open, or rather narrow for a wheelchair. For people who are confused, the environment may be unclear so that, even if they are physically able, they may not be able to find the toilet.

Clothing

Some types of clothing can be difficult to undo, for example because they are too tight or have fiddly buttons.

Drugs

Many medicines can interfere with the ability to keep continent. For example, diuretics are drugs that stimulate the production of more urine. They are prescribed for some heart conditions to get rid of extra, unwanted fluid. But with someone who is already at risk of incontinence they may be enough to start it off. Tranquillisers may create drowsiness which in turn may dull the person's sensation of having a full bladder.

Psychological changes

Depression, perhaps caused by bereavement, may lead to a sense of hopelessness and a 'couldn't care less' attitude to incontinence.

Caring for clients who are incontinent of urine

As a care worker, you need to adopt an optimistic approach to the problem of incontinence. Expect to bring about improvements. This will encourage clients to adopt a similar attitude and will minimise the damaging effects to morale and self-esteem.

Incidents of incontinence should be dealt with in a matter-of-fact way. Go to great lengths to avoid showing any revulsion towards the task of cleaning an incontinent person. Look on incontinence as a problem to be solved, not as a personal failing.

Restoring continence

Assessment is the first step towards a solution. Charts are available to record the progress of the client throughout the day. Once a reasonable period of time has elapsed, see whether there is any pattern to the incontinence which might then be used as the basis for helping the client restore continence. Discuss how this should be done with your local continence advisor – usually a specially trained nurse.

Visits to the toilet should be planned according to a systematic assessment of clients' needs. For some clients, a simple reminder will be sufficient; in other cases, you will need to give physical assistance. Always allow adequate time and privacy for each resident to use the toilet. Record the result on the assessment sheet.

Managing incontinence

Some clients cannot regain continence. In these situations, incontinence will have to be managed by means of an incontinence aid, such as an absorbent, padded garment, or a sheath fitted over the penis which conducts urine into a bag attached to the client's leg. The client remains incontinent but he or she need no longer be embarrassed by the consequences.

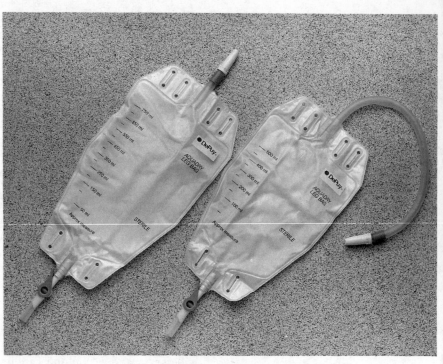

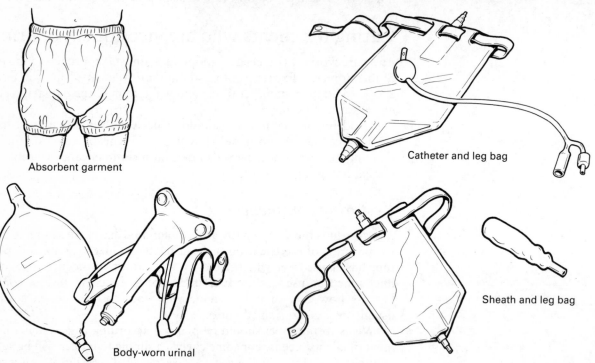

Absorbent garment

Catheter and leg bag

Body-worn urinal

Sheath and leg bag

ACTIVITY

Choose one client you know who suffers from incontinence of urine.

- What is the cause of this client's incontinence?
- How is it being dealt with?
- Are any special aids used?
- How would you describe the client's psychological

reactions to being incontinent?
- When caring for this client after he or she has been incontinent, how would you assess your own reaction?
- How do you think you would cope if *you* were incontinent? What would be the biggest problems you would face?

Causes of incontinence of faeces

Incontinence of faeces is less common than incontinence of urine. Even so, it is extremely distressing when it does occur. You need to be aware of just how upsetting this is to both clients and relatives, and be prepared to offer help and support. Always refer the problem to a medical practitioner, so that any underlying problem can be treated as soon as possible. There are several reasons why incontinence of faeces may occur.

Constipation

This appears an unlikely cause at first glance. What happens is that the rectum becomes blocked with faeces; this then leads to leakage around the blockage. Clothes are soiled continually by small amounts of soft faecal material. Whenever this occurs, always suspect constipation, and report your observations to your supervisor. The technical name for this kind of blockage is *impaction of faeces*.

Diarrhoea

Loose stools are harder to control than those that are normally formed. There are many reasons why diarrhoea occurs. Infections, inappropriate diet or too many laxatives are some of the possibilities.

Loss of control

Disorders of the nervous system – Alzheimer's disease, for example – can lead to clients losing control of their bowel movements. Instead of being able to resist the urge to go to the toilet, they may have no option but to open their bowels immediately – regardless of the time, place or circumstances.

Confusion and disorientation

Some clients fail to recognise where they are, or are confused about the correct time of day. When this happens, they may become incontinent of faeces.

Caring for clients who are incontinent of faeces

Assessment and medical help

Always refer clients to a doctor. It is essential that a proper medical assessment be made. Once this is done, you will need to help treat the cause.

Help clients to avoid constipation. Diet may need to be improved – see section 4.19 for more information on this. The doctor may prescribe laxatives or suppositories to help in the short term.

Managing incontinence

Good toilet habits will help clients to maintain regular bowel movements. Encourage clients to go to the toilet after each meal because this is when the body's natural reflexes are most active.

If incontinence occurs, do everything you can to minimise the embarrassment for the client. Carry out the various tasks – cleaning and making the client comfortable – with as little fuss as possible. Clothes will need to be laundered appropriately. Some areas have special laundry facilities to help clients who are incontinent – ask your local social services department. Dealing with faeces is unpleasant but you must not show disgust or reject the client by your manner. The best way to achieve this is to try to imagine what the client must be feeling.

Take advice from your local health authority continence advisor on the best way to prevent or manage future problems. In some cases, disposable incontinence aids are the only way of ensuring that clients stay reasonably comfortable. Clothing, too, needs to be suitable so that undressing and dressing is made easier.

Help relatives to talk about their particular concerns and distress. There are never any simple solutions, but most relatives and friends will take encouragement from seeing care workers deal with this most difficult of problems in a sensitive yet practical and matter-of-fact-way.

4.16 Meeting physical health-care needs: *Mobility and exercise*

Our sense of freedom is closely related to our physical freedom. While we remain fit and healthy, threats to our mobility often seem remote and irrelevant. However, the ageing process eventually reminds us all of just how much we take freedom of movement for granted.

Older people often remain mobile for many years. Entrants to the London marathon provide evidence for this. Nevertheless, there are large numbers of older clients for whom loss of mobility is a major problem.

Common causes of loss of mobility

Many factors contribute to reduced mobility – these are some:

- arthritis or rheumatism;
- painful feet;
- breathing problems;
- strokes;
- obesity;
- difficulty in seeing;
- heart and circulation problems;
- consequences of accidents;
- anxiety and depression;
- side-effects of medication – for instance, tranquillisers can lead to drowsiness.

As well as the person being unable to get around easily, loss of mobility creates other complications:

- clients are often afraid of falling;
- fewer social contacts may lead to loneliness and isolation;
- reduced environmental stimulation may result in serious sensory deprivation: this can lead to psychological problems, including apathy or restlessness;
- there are often psychological reactions, such as depression;
- the impact of dementia may be felt earlier or made worse.

Further physical complications may occur if mobility problems go unrecognised. Most importantly, *pressure sores* can develop rapidly, in places such as the sacrum (the bottom of the spine) and the heels. In the older person whose skin is losing elasticity, these ulcers can be very slow to heal. They create considerable discomfort and make mobility even more difficult to achieve. Always seek advice and assistance urgently from the general practitioner or community nurse if clients develop pressure sores or other ulcers.

Improving mobility

- *Aim to prevent mobility problems* If this is impossible, at least aim to stop them getting worse.
- *Use exercise programmes* Exercise is a matter for the whole body. Even someone who is seated for most of the day (due to paralysis, perhaps) must exercise joints and muscles regularly and systematically.

- *Use mobility aids when necessary* These include walking frames, for example. Physiotherapists or occupational therapists will advise on the best equipment and how to use it.

- *Encourage appropriate footware* This should be comfortable, the correct size and suited to the conditions. Don't, for example, expect a client to be able to walk any distance in slippers.

- *Make movement as easy as possible* Analyse the everyday movements the client needs to make. Ask yourself where he or she needs to move in the course of the day. Review whether, for instance, clients can easily get into and out of chairs and beds, and on to and off toilets. Are chairs arranged in a helpful way – close enough to the toilets, for example?

- *Encourage clients and staff to think positively* Mobility and exercise are important issues for all older clients, whether they remain active or are apparently very limited in their movements. A positive attitude on the part of the staff is essential and will help clients to be more confident and optimistic.

Lifting

Sometimes you will need to move clients – from bed to chair, from chair to chair, to sit them up in bed or to help them to stand up from a chair. Sadly, many care workers suffer chronic pain and disability due to back injuries as a result of not using proper lifting techniques. Under the Health and Safety Act 1974 you have an obligation to take reasonable care of yourself and others who might be affected by what you do. Never risk your health by trying to lift anyone or anything without being absolutely sure that you know the correct way. Lifting is a skill that you must learn from an experienced care worker who has received special training. Remember these important principles:

- give yourself space;
- stand close;

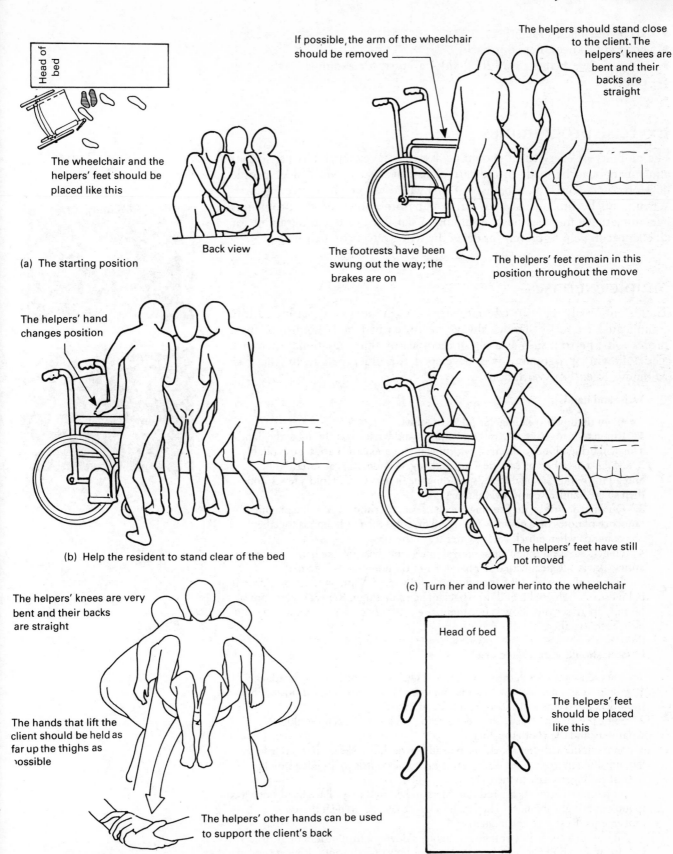

Head of bed

The wheelchair and the helpers' feet should be placed like this

(a) The starting position

Back view

If possible, the arm of the wheelchair should be removed

The helpers should stand close to the client. The helpers' knees are bent and their backs are straight

The footrests have been swung out the way; the brakes are on

The helpers' feet remain in this position throughout the move

The helpers' hand changes position

(b) Help the resident to stand clear of the bed

The helpers' feet have still not moved

(c) Turn her and lower her into the wheelchair

The helpers' knees are very bent and their backs are straight

The hands that lift the client should be held as far up the thighs as possible

The helpers' other hands can be used to support the client's back

Head of bed

The helpers' feet should be placed like this

The two-person lift, used to transfer a client from a bed to a wheelchair

- keep your back straight;
- bend your knees, not your back;
- always use a helper or a lifting aid – a hoist, for example – when you can.

Exercise programmes

The mobility of every client should be assessed at regular intervals, so that adjustments can be made to the care plan if necessary. Most older people develop some degree of arthritis, but this will often not be noticed at first. When joints become increasingly stiff and painful, however, the problem is beginning to get more seriously disabling. A sensible exercise programme for all clients can help to prevent or delay the worst effects of arthritis.

Simple exercises

These can easily be carried out each day in any care setting. More complicated exercises should always be prescribed and monitored by a professional person, such as a physiotherapist or an occupational therapist. The following programme was developed for older people by the East Midlands Keep-Fit Association.

Wrist and hands

To maintain mobility in fingers and wrist joints:
1   Rub hands together. Massage the fingers and wrists. Gently shake the hands. This will bring blood to the area, warming it and make the hands more pliable.
2   Make a fist, then spread the hand and fingers wide. Repeat several times. Spread the hands flat on a table, spreading the fingers wide. Hold a few seconds, then shake hands. Repeat several times.
3   On a hard surface, do five-finger exercises across and back – like playing a sequence of notes on a piano. Single hand first and then both hands together. Shake hands when muscles ache. Later try in the air.
4   Fingers relaxed, rotate wrist several times clockwise. Shake hand and repeat anticlockwise. Repeat with other hand. Later try both hands together.
5   Sit on a chair with feet flat on floor, slightly apart. With hand relaxed drop it palm down on thigh; lift and drop back of hand on thigh. Repeat several times, taking care to see the elbow is free to move easily. Try each hand separately and later both together.

Elbows, shoulders, neck and head

To relax tense muscles in the shoulders and neck which often cause headaches:
1   Stand or sit on a chair, with arms hanging easily downwards at sides. Lift shoulders up to ears and allow them to drop. Repeat.
2   Same position as No. 1. Shoulder circling backwards, each shoulder separately and then both together.
3   Sit or stand with feet apart. Drop head forward, roll slowly in a circle to the left, finishing in front, head down. Press neck backwards to lift head slowly. Repeat rolling in circle to the right.
4   Sit with hands on knees, and shoulders and elbows easy. Turn head sideways to look over right shoulder. Then turn to look over left. Repeat these movements. Rest and repeat again.
5   Sit tall on a chair. Lift both arms slightly sideways, turn insides of arms to face front, and pull backwards; relax arms so they drop to sides. Repeat several times.

Feet and ankles

To strengthen feet and leg muscles (for maximum benefit these exercises should be done barefoot or in stockinged feet):
1 Sit on the front half of a chair, holding two front corners for support. Sole of foot brushing the floor forward and backward several times. Repeat with other foot. Allow foot to be easy and loose.
2 Position as in No. 1. Lift heel as high as possible and lower. Several times with each foot, then both together.
3 Tap foot lightly with toe, lift foot and tap lightly with heel. Repeat several times with each foot.
4 Sit on a chair with heel resting on another chair or stool. Keep heel on the spot and circle big toe, outwards and round trying to increase the size of the circle. Repeat with other foot. Both heels resting on stool or chair, slightly apart. Circle both big toes inwards towards each other, increasing size of circle.

Knee and hip

The following exercises will help to maintain or improve the range of these joints and the power of the muscles:
1 Sit on the front half of a chair, hold two front corners for support. Lift knee as high as possible, then return foot to floor. Repeat with the other knee. Repeat these movements several times.
2 Lift one foot off the floor, move leg outwards to place foot on floor at side of chair. Lift and return it to the other one. Repeat several times lifting leg as high and as far to side as possible. Repeat with other leg.
3 Sitting sideways on chair, grip the chair back with one hand and the front corner of the seat with the other. Put the feet on the floor, with one slightly in front of the other. Lift both feet off the floor at the same time, then return them to the floor. It helps to lean backwards with the body when lifting and forwards slightly when lowering. Gradually increase this lean so that weight goes on to the feet each time. From this rhythmic movement it is easy to stand, steadying the balance with the hand on the chair.

> (From *Take Care of Yourself* by Fiona von Zwanenberg,
> published by Help the Aged, 1988.
> Reproduced by kind permission of the Winslow Press and Help the Aged.)

ACTIVITY

1 Review the clients in your care who have mobility problems. Try to find the causes. Do they all fit into the list in this section? If not, do you know what the missing causes are?

2 Choose a small group of clients. Try out some of the exercises suggested in this section.

Finding out more . . .

★ The Disabled Living Foundation is a national source of information on the different kinds of aids and equipment for people with disabilities which includes mobility problems. Contact details can be found on page 149.
★ Arthritis Care is a national voluntary organisation working with people with arthritis. Amongst a range of activities, it provides information and advice, and publishes helpful leaflets. Details from: Arthritis Care, 5 Grosvenor Crescent, London SW1X 7ER (071–235 0902).

4.17 Meeting physical health-care needs: *Care of the feet*

As the previous section has shown, healthy feet are essential to staying mobile. Pain and disorders of the feet generally make walking increasingly difficult and will aggravate other problems, such as shortness of breath or heart failure. The combined effect of these is often to demoralise the client, leading to a reluctance to try to stay active and mobile. There are many reasons, then, why you should make foot care a high priority.

Without special training, the care offered should be no more than that which would be carried out as part of a normal hygiene and bathing routine. Any needs that the client may have beyond these should be dealt with by a state-registered chiropodist. For example, refer these situations to a chiropodist:

- nails overgrown or ingrowing;
- swelling or colour changes in the feet;
- past history of foot problems;
- corns – a hardening of the skin on the toes (avoid the 'corn cures' from the chemist);
- bunions – inflamed swellings of the first joint of the big toe;
- diabetic client – nerve damage can cause numbness and may mean that the client will not be able to feel pain and discomfort; also the blood supply is often reduced, resulting in slow healing and possibly the death of tissue (gangrene).

Preventing problems

Chiropodists are in short supply in most areas of the NHS. Although older people are entitled to treatment under the NHS, many go to private chiropodists, if they can afford to, because waiting lists are often long. Care homes, day centres and domiciliary workers should do all they can to cope with this shortage of professional help. For example:

- you should build up a knowledge of local chiropody services, so that clients can be given this information when they need it;
- you should develop an effective relationship with local chiropodists, so that they became more aware of the needs of the clients, and the skills of the staff, in your particular care setting;
- as a care worker, do everything you can to help clients to prevent problems – this means being aware of the circumstances which can cause potential problems.

As explained earlier, diabetes is one illness that puts the feet at special risk. There are others.

The feet can become damaged whenever sensation is lost – if clients cannot feel pain, they will not know when injury has occurred. Strokes and multiple sclerosis can cause this. Swollen feet is another common complaint amongst older clients. This can be caused by serious heart disease, in which the body's pump becomes less efficient and fluid collects in the feet and ankles. However, it is just as likely to be caused by posture and movement, such as sitting in the same position for hours on end. Clients who are confused and restless may also suffer from this problem – again because of the effects of gravity. It is generally a good idea to encourage clients to put their feet up regularly to give the circulation a chance to clear away any

ACTIVITY

1 When you next help to bathe clients, take particular notice of the state of their feet. Think about these questions.

- In what ways do the feet of older clients differ from those of younger people?
- What are the common problems that older people have in looking after their own feet?
- Which parts of the feet are particularly troublesome? Ask clients what they feel about this.
- How can you improve foot care in your own work setting?

2 Discuss these questions with your supervisor and colleagues.

excess fluid that has collected in the feet and ankles. Remember, however, that with clients who suffer from heart disease, you should always follow the instructions given by the doctor or nurse attending the client.

Good general foot care and hygiene will go a long way to preventing problems. You should encourage or carry out the following simple precautions:

- Wash the feet once a day and dry them carefully.
- Check the feet when washing for any accidental damage.
- Make sure that shoes fit well. Ask the assistant to measure foot length and width every time a client buys a new pair – with increasing age, feet do not necessarily stay exactly the same shape.
- Treat dry feet and hard skin using a moisturiser, such as a favourite hand lotion. Rub this in all over the feet once a day. There is no need to apply it between the toes; these areas are usually already moist.
- Encourage the client to avoid becoming overweight. Every extra ounce means extra work for the feet and joints. This precaution will help to reduce foot problems and minimise the effects of arthritis.
- Deal with small injuries – grazes, scratches or small blisters – by covering them with sterile gauze and bandaging or fixing the gauze with hypoallergenic tape. Never prick a blister – the risk of infection is high. Change the dressing each day and arrange to see the chiropodist or doctor if the wound has not healed within two or three days.
- Cut the toenails regularly.

Cutting toenails

This skill should be learnt from a competent person at first hand. Many older clients have nails that are thickened and hard. If you are at all worried, raise your concerns with your supervisor before proceeding. Some clients will need their feet inspected by a state-registered chiropodist before it is safe to cut the nails. The procedure is as follows:

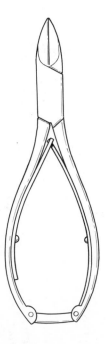

- Make the client comfortable, with the foot resting on a stool. The ideal time is after a bath when the nails are softer.
- You should be sitting low down, and should ensure that the light is good. Wear protective clothing and rest the client's foot on a paper towel before starting.
- Both the nail nippers and nail file should be sterile before use. Before cutting nails, wash your hands with an antiseptic lotion.
- Clean the foot with an appropriate antiseptic (for example, sterile cottonwool soaked in 0.5 per cent Chlorhexidine in 70 per cent alcohol).
- Cut the nails straight across, using chiropodist's nail nippers. Leave the nails level with the soft part of the toe. It is safer for you to leave them too long than too short.
- Do not cut down the sides of the nail.
- Gently file rough edges with a nail file.

Where possible, encourage clients to look after their own feet. Some clients will not be capable of this due to their inability to hold the nippers safely or to reach. Nevertheless, involve clients as far as possible. Clients from certain ethnic groups – Muslims, for example – place very great importance on modesty and in keeping the body covered. It is important to check and agree with the client what would be an acceptable way of carrying out foot care.

4.18 Meeting physical health-care needs: *Eating and drinking*

Meals and meal-times

Meal-times have both a nutritional and a social purpose – and care workers in residential and day-care settings need to keep both in mind. As well as ensuring that clients receive a nutritious diet, you should make the occasion as enjoyable as possible. There are several points to think about here:

- the timing of meals;
- seating arrangements;
- the choice of menu;
- variety to suit different cultural groups;
- meeting individual needs and preferences;
- special diets, such as diabetic, low-carbohydrate or softer foods;
- help with eating – using eating aids, or feeding clients;
- health education – how far should better eating habits be encouraged?

Each care setting will have its own needs and constraints. However, whatever the particular circumstances, meal-times offer a great opportunity for creativity in care. This applies equally to the diet itself and to the social aspects of the meal.

Nutritional needs of older people

Older people need to adapt their food and fluid intake to their changed needs:

- The need for energy foods (carbohydrates and fats) is lower because older people are generally less active. However, the danger is that not only these nutrients will be reduced but others also.
- Other nutrients – proteins, vitamins and minerals – are needed in amounts similar to those for younger adults. However, most of us use too much salt in our diet. It is good practice for older people to try to limit this because too much salt encourages high blood pressure. Alternatively, use a low-sodium salt substitute.
- Fibre is essential to a healthy diet, in helping to prevent constipation.
- Many older people tend to drink less than they should. This may be because they are frightened of incontinence, or because they want to avoid having to go to the toilet during the night. The advice should always be to drink at least two litres every day. A good fluid intake will avoid dehydration and also go some way to preventing constipation.

Clients at risk

Are older people particularly vulnerable to problems with diet? Every stage of life has its own risks and old age is no exception. Nutritional problems may be linked to medical and social factors that are particularly common in old age. Medical factors include:

- breathlessness, as in chronic bronchitis;
- depression;
- difficulty in swallowing;
- poor teeth or dentures.

Social factors include:

- being housebound;
- living alone, especially for men;
- bereavement;
- poverty.

When clients are affected by several of these risk factors, the chances of poor nutrition are significantly higher. If you visit older people in their own homes, pay particular attention to your clients' nutritional state, and to his or her social and medical circumstances. As well as giving a clue to the dietary needs of clients, the factors listed here may also help to indicate other potential problems. They should be included in every client's assessment.

Cultural variations

Care workers need to know about appropriate diets for clients from different cultural or religious backgrounds. In some cases certain foods may be prohibited. Get to know more about the subject by talking to clients and their relatives. Where there is a high proportion of clients from a particular ethnic group, make contact with local community leaders who will often be able to provide information and advice on the best way to meet special dietary needs.

However, avoid the mistake of thinking that every individual from a particular culture will automatically want one particular diet all the time. Don't forget, either, that some of these foods can be equally appealing to clients from quite different backgrounds. Think how popular curry, sweet-and-sour pork and kebabs have become in recent years. Old age does not mean that experimentation is over and done with. Some of the spicier foods, for instance, may be just what is needed when taste buds have become less sensitive. Encourage clients to experiment with their diet by introducing changes.

ACTIVITY

1 Eating is a very personal activity. Habits form early in our lives and tend to stick. Observe and analyse your own eating habits.

- Are you a fast or a slow eater?
- Do you eat in a particular sequence, for example vegetables before the meat, or vice versa?
- Do you always mix foods in each mouthful?
- Do you save the tastiest foods until the end?

2 Discuss this with several colleagues. How can this exercise help you to care better for your clients?

ACTIVITY

Care workers often have to help older clients with eating. The help may be no more than cutting up food. On the other hand, for clients who are severely disabled or confused it could include the whole of the feeding process. The only way you will really get to understand this experience is to try it out for yourself. It is time very well spent.

With the agreement of your supervisor, arrange a role-play. Together with a colleague, take it in turns to feed and be fed. Be as realistic as possible. If you can, use the normal dining room. The clients may wonder what you are up to but are unlikely to object to the free entertainment! Try out several variations, such as these:

- vary the speed of feeding;
- use larger or smaller pieces of food;
- try feeding your colleague from a standing and a sitting position;
- vary the sequence of different foods;
- try holding a conversation with your colleague at the same time.

ACTIVITY

Think about the meal arrangements for clients. With colleagues, discuss the following questions:

- What are the seating arrangements for main meals?
- How long have they been like this?
- Do clients talk much to each other during a meal?
- What type of tables are used? Are they ideal?

- Who decides where clients sit? Is it based on the free choice of the clients, the kind of diet, physical abilities . . . or what?
- Can you think of ways in which you could make meal-times more enjoyable for clients?

Reading on . . .

★ For specific guidance on the diets of different cultures, contact the National Extension College (see page 149), which produces several useful handbooks and resource packs.

4.19 Meeting physical health-care needs: *Problems of nutrition*

There are many ways in which care workers can help to prevent or improve dietary problems. However, a professional dietitian's advice should always be sought whenever a client's eating or drinking is causing real concern.

Obesity

Obesity develops when the body is taking in more calories than it is using up. Excess calories are converted into fat and stored. For older people there are several hazards in being overweight:

- Movement becomes more difficult – for example getting in and out of chairs, dressing and bathing.
- Constipation may occur when there is little or no exercise.
- Extra strain on the joints may encourage arthritis.
- High blood pressure (often called *hypertension*) is more likely, and this can lead to heart failure and breathlessness.
- Accidents are more frequent.

'No, you can't have a Mars-a-day . . .'

Dealing with obesity

Try to prevent the problem in the first place by encouraging a properly balanced diet that contains a moderate number of calories. However, this may not be possible. Often, clients have built up their body weight a long while before they need care. Other clients may have a very sweet tooth and resist all attempts at change.

If your clients are not suffering from obvious disabilities related to obesity, there is probably no need to try to treat the problem specifically. However, good advice on diet should always be offered.

Where some action is needed, clients should be encouraged to cut down on fat and sugar – but the reductions should only be moderate, never drastic. There is a great danger that, if too much is cut out too quickly, essential nutrients will become deficient.

Sufficient exercise is as important as diet. Exercise burns up calories and helps to improve the function of the heart and lungs, prevents constipation, and keeps joints supple.

Insufficient diet (undernutrition)

There are many reasons why clients fail to eat and drink adequately and so become undernourished:

- confusion and dementia – clients are often unable to concentrate sufficiently to prepare or eat a meal, and may not be able to communicate clearly when they are unwell;
- dental problems, for example no teeth or dentures, or gum disease;
- poor appetite, perhaps due to physical illness or depression (appetite can be quite an accurate indicator of mood and feeling – see section 4.24);
- emotional crisis, such as bereavement;
- social isolation, leading to apathy and lack of interest.

Serious cases of poor nutrition are relatively uncommon amongst older people. Where the problem is a shortage of nutrients, the most commonly affected are calcium, vitamin B and occasionally iron. Some people are prone to a shortage of vitamin D, which is obtained in two ways: from the diet and as a result of the action of sunshine on the skin. Asian women, for example, who traditionally spend a lot of their time in the house, are particularly prone to this deficiency, especially if their diet is inadequate in vitamin D in the first place.

Counteract problems by encouraging clients to eat well-balanced and varied diets. Exactly what this means for any particular client depends on her or his individual preferences, background and culture.

Insufficient fluids (dehydration)

Older clients often drink too little. When this occurs, it can seriously affect the working of the kidneys and bladder. Infections and incontinence may result. Clients should be encouraged to drink at least two litres of fluid each day. Alcohol is unhelpful in preventing dehydration, however, because it stimulates the kidneys to pass out *more* water and so can make the problem worse. With clients who are inclined to be incontinent of urine at night, care workers should arrange the drinking pattern to avoid large quantities in the few hours immediately before bedtime. Nevertheless, it is essential that the total quantity taken for the day is sufficient. Patience and an attractive selection of drinks is necessary. Try to adapt the clients' existing patterns rather than abruptly changing the habits of a lifetime – offer herbal teas, for example. This is where a thorough individual care assessment comes into its own.

Constipation

One of the most important factors in causing constipation is a diet low in fibre. This can be improved by eating more fruit and vegetables, wholemeal bread and high-fibre breakfast cereals. Many attractive high-fibre foods are now widely available. Fluids should be increased at the same time.

However, diet is not the whole story. Encouraging more exercise will help stimulate bowel movements, as well as benefiting most other systems of the body.

Hidden problems

Difficulties with eating and drinking can still arise even when clients are in residential or day care. If meals become merely routine events, there is always the danger that no one will realise that clients are not eating and drinking as much as they need to. For this reason, you should regularly review each client's eating and drinking.

ACTIVITY

1 Choose a client and keep a diary of his or her food and fluid intake for a week. Wherever possible, ask the client to do this, explaining why. Keep the same diary for yourself and ask one or two colleagues to do the same.

2 At the end of the week, compare the different diaries. What are the similarities and differences:

- in the kinds of foods eaten and fluids drunk?
- in the timing of meals?

You will probably find many differences. For instance, you and your colleagues may be able to choose when you have meals, whereas clients in residential and day care often have much less control. Do these differences matter? Discuss this with your supervisor and colleagues.

Reading on . . .

★ *Eating a Way into the 90s* is a booklet published in 1988 by the British Diatetic Association's Nutrition Advisory Group for the Elderly. It is described as 'a handbook for those concerned with providing meals for the elderly' and is valuable for care workers in residential, day and domiciliary care. It packs a lot into a few pages.

4.20   Meeting physical health-care needs: *Personal hygiene*

Hygiene is important at all stages of life. However, older people often have to contend with insensitive and inaccurate social stereotypes, such as the idea that 'old' means 'smelly'. As a care worker, you should do all you can to reject and counteract these negative stereotypes. The best way to do so is to ensure that they are never true.

Helping with physical needs is one of the most challenging aspects of personal care. It is fraught with difficulties for many reasons. For instance, the thought of helping to bathe an older person can be very traumatic if you are young and new to the job. 'How will the client react? How will I react?' Yet care workers need to avoid the danger of paralysis through being too self-conscious.

Clients often find it highly embarrassing to expose certain parts of the body, especially to care workers of the opposite sex. For some clients – Muslim women, for example – this involves religious beliefs. Even for the experienced care worker there can be some pitfalls. In this case, the question may be how to maintain high-quality personal care, day in and day out. Bathing and other personal activities can soon become mere chores to be carried out as quickly and as easily as possible. Routine can become more important than the client. However dedicated and competent you may be, you have to face this. At times, physical care can be simply exhausting. And remembering the individuality of the client can then be an awesome task.

One way of dealing with potential problems of this kind is to ensure that clients are allowed to be as independent as possible in all aspects of their physical care. If assessment has been carried out thoroughly, staff should have a good idea of the preferences and needs of each client.

Baths, showers and washing

We all have our own individual standards of personal cleanliness. As a care worker, you need to respect the wishes of individual clients while encouraging a socially acceptable level of hygiene. In some cases, clients may have let themselves slide into a state of poor hygiene over a period, perhaps through loneliness and lack of motivation. Where this is the situation, the clients' self-esteem and self-respect will need attention. Feeling clean and well turned out contributes greatly to helping people feel better about themselves.

There can be considerable cultural variations in approaches to cleanliness. Clients from the hotter parts of the world often wish to wash only in running water, regarding baths as unhygienic. They may also wish to have a shower or strip wash twice a day. If no shower is available, some clients may prefer to use a jug to pour water over themselves. This can be carried out in the bath. Assistance may be needed with this. Likewise, toilet paper is seen by many as unhygienic. For these clients, a jug of warm water should be provided so that they can wash themselves after using the toilet.

Being prepared

All toiletries should be easily accessible before a bath or shower. Work out what is needed in advance and gather the items together. Because of a tendency to dry skin, Afro-Caribbean clients may wish to use creams or lotions after a bath. Have these ready.

Always allow enough time. Clients will differ in their needs. Some will regard the bath as a place to relax as well as get clean. Others prefer to be in and out as soon as possible. In residential and day care there are bound to be occasions when there will be great pressure on staff availability. If staff time is severely restricted it is better to be honest with clients and explain the position. In this way staff will gain more respect and most clients will feel involved.

Water temperature

Don't rely on your elbow to measure the temperature of bath water. Always check this with a special bath thermometer. If in doubt make it too cool rather than too hot. There have been a number of tragedies where older people in care have been severely scalded in the bath.

All showers used in care settings should have clearly marked temperature controls and these should be adjusted to suit the preferences of the clients.

Getting in and getting out

Take-off and landing are the most vulnerable times for airline passengers. Similarly, getting in and out of the bath represent moments of particular risk. Hoists are often available and should always be used when clients are unable to step into and out of the bath. However, it has been known for expensive pieces of machinery to stand idle while staff struggle unnecessarily. Inadequate training in the use of hoists is sometimes to blame. All care workers should ensure that they are competent in the operation of whatever lifting equipment is available. Supervisors will be able to provide the instruction needed. It is worth remembering that clients may not have the same faith as you in the technology – introduce the procedure step-by-step and with confidence. Non-slip mats in the bath and shower will give greater assurance to most clients, as will hand grips in strategic positions. Robust shower and bath seats can also be used to increase the safety of clients, and ease the strain on staff.

Observation

A bath or shower is a good opportunity to observe a client's condition, and take appropriate actions. For example:

- *Skin condition* Are there any rashes or sores; any lumps or other unexpected marks?
- *Nails* If these need cutting, immediately after a bath or shower is the best time, as they will be softer then.
- *Communication* Physical intimacy encourages psychological intimacy. A bath can be a time when clients get worries off their chests. Care workers should be prepared for this eventuality and know how to deal with it and to use it.

Facial hair

Many older women find the growth of facial hair an embarrassment. You can do much to improve the morale of clients by attending to this, either by shaving or using hair-removing creams. Occasionally, some clients will not want this done. However much staff may disagree, clients clearly have a perfect right to choose on matters of this kind.

4.21 Meeting physical health-care needs: *Getting up and getting dressed*

Getting up and getting dressed is much more than just the start to the day. It is also an indication of how independent we are. If it goes well then the rest of the day seems to follow suit. If not, and we 'get out of the wrong side of the bed', the day takes on a gloomy tone. We feel tired and others often find us grumpy and unsociable.

Older clients whose independence has been threatened by disability or illness face particular problems at this point in the day. In everyday life, the ability to get dressed is often used to mark the end of a period of illness. Many of us can remember from childhood the relief when Mum or Dad relented and said finally, 'All right, you can get up today, your temperature is down now.'

Dressing difficulties

There are many reasons why older clients may find dressing more difficult than it used to be. For example:

- *Arthritic joints* may not work so well as they did, making it hard to carry out many aspects of dressing – handling buttons, for example, or lifting the arms above the head.
- *Weakness or paralysis of one or more limbs* will create unusual problems for clients, for example the weakness of the arm and leg on one side of the body that can occur after a stroke.
- *Heart or breathing problems* can cause tiredness and breathlessness.
- *Mental confusion* may prevent clients recognising their clothes or being able to coordinate their movements adequately.

Choosing clothes

It should go without saying that clients have the right to choose their own clothes. However, you have to put this into practice under conditions that may not be ideal. Choice will be limited by cost. Clients who are living on very little income may have to explore ways of getting the best value for money. Care workers can help by finding sources of good secondhand clothes. Clients who keep in regular contact with relatives may receive financial help from them. But this will not always be possible.

When caring for clients from different ethnic origins, you will need to find out their particular clothing needs – for example, many Hindu and Muslim women wear a sari over an underskirt and blouse. You will need to learn how best to help clients who wear clothes which are unfamiliar to you. Where there are no immediate relatives or friends available for advice, you should try to enlist the help of local people in the community who share the same ethnic background.

Helping clients with dressing

A proper assessment is the best start. Where clients have more than the simplest of problems, contact the local occupational therapist so that she or he can carry out a detailed dressing assessment. Following this, it should be possible to match the help given to the specific needs of the clients.

How much direct help should you give? It's a difficult question, and one that depends on the needs of the individual client. Nevertheless, the help provided should be only what the client needs, and no more. It is the easiest thing in the world to do too much in order to save time. Taking everyday responsibilities away from clients can remove their skills and confidence too. The level of direct help to be given should be discussed with colleagues and negotiated with clients.

Minimising the amount of direct help is not at all the same thing as abandoning the clients to their own devices. You should stay with the clients while they are re-learning these skills, offering advice and encouragement. Allow sufficient time. Concentrate on the clients' main learning needs, so that help can be directed at these specifically.

Dressing tips

Generally, if clients can stay sitting up without assistance, they should be able to dress themselves.

- Make sure there are mirrors available. These should be large enough, close enough and at the correct height.
- Encourage clients to dress while sitting on the side of the bed, rather than standing.
- Encourage them to dress the weak arm or leg first. For example, they should put the affected arm into the sleeve of cardigans or shirts first, followed by the good arm.
- With trousers, try clipping the pants inside the trousers with clothes pegs. Both can then be put on together.
- If balance is a problem, clients can try putting on pants, trousers and socks while still in bed. Then they can swing round and sit up.
- Bras can have Velcro front openings. (Velcro is a self-fastening material that is widely available and often used in clothes for people with disabilities.)
- Skirts can be made wrap-over, and fastened with Velcro.
- Slip-on shoes might be easier than lace-ups.
- Try neckties that don't need knotting each time. Clip-on versions can be bought. Alternatively, sew in elastic behind the knot, so that the tie can be slipped on over the head.
- Make the best use of specialist dressing aids – for example, long shoehorns for clients who cannot reach down far enough to use the normal size, or dressing hooks which let clients lift clothes over an impaired arm or shoulder.

ACTIVITY

1 Analyse your own getting-up and dressing routines. Try to answer these questions:

- How do you feel when you wake up? Can you explain why?
- How long does it take you to get up and get ready to go out?
- What are the stages in this process? List them in the order they occur.

2 When you have done this, analyse the routines of clients by comparing them with your own list. Try it out on one or two clients in your care. How do their routines differ from your own? How much of the difference is due to:

- clients' individual differences (including differences due to disability) and preferences?
- the restrictions of the care environment?

3 Discuss your findings with your supervisor and colleagues. Are there ways in which you can improve your care practice?

4.22 Meeting physical health-care needs: *Keeping warm*

At either end of life, the human body is particularly vulnerable to temperature changes. As children, we are blithely unaware of this. However, when we reach more advanced years we need to understand the processes involved because of the considerable dangers of allowing our body temperature to fall too low. This condition is known as *hypothermia*.

Hypothermia

Normal body temperature is around 37 degrees Celsius (98.4 degrees Fahrenheit), although older people usually have slightly lower normal temperatures. Hypothermia is defined as a body temperature lower than 35 degrees Celsius (95 degrees Fahrenheit). Death usually occurs when the body temperature falls below 26 degrees Celsius (75 degrees Fahrenheit). The person gradually becomes unconscious and death is due to heart and lung failure.

The usual reason for hypothermia is exposure to cold. Every winter in Britain, up to one million older people are at risk. But why should this be? Important reasons are:

- *Failure to feel and react to cold* Shivering (which is a way of raising body temperature) is less efficient, too.
- *Reduced mobility* Less heat is generated through movement.
- *Financial difficulties* Clients may try to economise by reducing heating (normally one of the largest household bills). The consequences are worse in houses that are poorly insulated.
- *Living alone* There is no one to call for help in an emergency.
- *Getting up to visit the toilet and insomnia* are both commoner amongst older people. The risk of a fall is greater.

Care workers who visit older clients in their own homes, and those who work in day centres, need to be especially alert to the possibility of hypothermia. In residential care, hypothermia should not arise under normal circumstances. However, some buildings are not easy to heat evenly and there can be cold areas. Should a client fall out of bed and this be unnoticed by staff for some time, there could be the risk that the body temperature might fall to a dangerous level.

When caring for older people who are suffering from dementia or confusion, special precautions have to be taken to minimise the risk of their walking out and having a fall in some remote spot. Should this occur in winter, there is a considerable risk of death. Section 4.26 covers this problem in detail.

Signs of hypothermia

- The skin feels cold to the touch.
- The client looks pale and there is usually some blueness visible on the lips, ears or fingers.
- Confusion is followed by increasing drowsiness and, finally, unconsciousness.

Treatment of hypothermia

- Send for medical help or call an ambulance.
- Remove any wet clothing.
- Re-warm the client gradually. No attempt should be made to speed up this process. It may take several hours to restore a normal body temperature.
- Warm the bedroom to 25–30 degrees Celsius. The bed should be warmed with hot-water bottles or an electric blanket, but these should be removed before the person is put into bed.
- Bedclothes should be lightweight.
- Reassure the person by your presence and by talking gently.
- Give a warm drink to sip. Never use alcohol because it increases blood flow to the skin and even more heat is lost.

Preventing hypothermia

The following points are particularly important in caring for clients at home, but many are relevant to residential care also.

- *Keeping warm* Heat the bedroom and shut windows. If this is impossible, think of moving the bed into a room where an adequate temperature can be maintained. The target should be 25 degrees Celsius. The bed should not be against an outside wall.
- *Safety* Reduce the risk of falls by installing good lighting, safe floor coverings and handrails. Avoid trailing electric leads.
- *Clothing* Clothing should consist of several layers, but take care to avoid a top layer that is so tight that it could restrict movements and possibly blood flow. Natural fibres are better than synthetic. The head is a major source of heat loss and should be covered at night. Bed socks and gloves might also be worn.
- *Help in emergencies* There should be a telephone within reach of the bed. Alarms can be fitted and, at the very least, a walking stick should be near to hand to bang on a wall or window.
- *Food* Sufficient food should be available to cover periods when the weather does not allow shopping. Warm drinks and hot meals are important.
- *Exercise* Indoor exercises should be carried out. These help the blood to circulate and generate heat.
- *Visits* Regular visits by relatives, friends and neighbours should be arranged. In bitter weather, it is wise to make several visits a day. If a rota can be agreed, the strain on any one person can be minimised.
- *Financial support* Advice should be offered about the various social security benefits that might be available to assist with heating, clothing and so on. Details can be obtained from social security offices or a Citizens' Advice Bureau. Problems should be referred to a social worker for professional advice.

ACTIVITY

Contact your local Department of Social Security. Ask them to let you have information about the kind of help available for older people at risk from hypothermia.

ACTIVITY

This activity is mainly for care workers in domiciliary or day care. If you work in residential care, you might be able to apply the exercise to residents' older relatives.

1 Ask clients about how they cope with winter. Try to choose individuals who you feel might be particularly vulnerable. Consider ways in which you could help to reduce this risk.

2 Discuss your findings with colleagues and your supervisor. Try to devise a care plan to deal with the potential problems.

4.23 Meeting physical health-care needs: *Resting and sleeping*

To 'get a good night's sleep' is to wake up refreshed and ready for the day. Unfortunately, many older people complain of poor sleep and there are certainly some changes in later years that help to explain this.

First, it is normal for older people to sleep less at one stretch at night. They often wake up earlier in the morning and find themselves with these early hours to fill either with constructive activity or brooding worries.

Secondly, it seems that the total amount of sleep that older people actually achieve is much the same as younger people – it is just that the distribution is different. Older people are inclined to take naps in the day which, to some extent, make up for the sleep lost at night.

Thirdly, older people tend to wake more at night because of disability or illness. For instance, pains in the joints can be a problem, as can the need to get up frequently to pass urine.

Conditions affecting sleep

Clients who enter residential care have to adapt to many things. Changes to their bedtime routines and rituals are some of the trickiest to cope with. Without the familiarity of their usual environment they find it difficult to relax and get off to sleep. Adapting to a different set of conditions inevitably takes time.

Noise

Older people are more susceptible to noise at night and are more likely to be woken up by telephones, doors banging, chattering voices and noises made by other residents. Unfortunately, staff who work at night may be less sensitive to these irritating noises – an understandable reaction but one that needs to be guarded against. The growing trend to providing single rooms in care homes will ease this problem but will not remove it altogether.

Temperature

Care homes are often heated to a level above that normally found in clients' own homes. Many people prefer to sleep in cooler conditions – some older people living at home cannot afford to heat rooms adequately in the first place. Clients should be able to adjust radiators in their own rooms to suit their personal preferences.

Lighting

While some people are accustomed to sleeping in pitch darkness, others prefer to have a light on for security or safety reasons. Care homes are required to maintain a low level of lighting at night in case of emergency. The light fittings themselves are usually confined to communal areas, such as hallways, but the light itself is often visible under doors or between curtains. This can be extremely annoying to some clients. Care workers should do all they can to resolve these problems without jeopardising the overall safety of clients.

Commercially available night lights, fitted in bedrooms, will help clients who dislike sleeping in pitch darkness.

Day activity

As a result of changed routine, disability or illness, many clients will be hard pressed to maintain their previous levels of activity. This in turn will affect sleep patterns. Poor sleep at night might be caused by too little exercise in the day, boredom and taking naps. By contrast, too much activity can lead to exhaustion and stress, bringing on worry which prevents sleep. Vigorous exercise just before going to bed can also make sleep more difficult.

Diet

There is no magic formula or special brew that will bring about natural and instant sleep. Hot milky drinks do help to some extent. What is most important is to maintain as far as possible the client's usual eating and drinking pattern. Of course, if past patterns have been responsible for sleep problems, then you will need to discuss with clients whether they wish to change them. It is well known that the caffeine in coffee can disrupt sleep and this effect worsens with age. Alcohol, in more than small quantities, can also cause sleep to be disturbed.

Worry and anxiety

Worries usually make it difficult to get to sleep. Be alert to the concerns of clients so that you can minimise sleep difficulties. Time taken in the evening to talk over worries with clients is time well spent. Sometimes these anxieties are fairly specific and can be dealt with there and then. In other cases, they are much more general. Nevertheless, time to talk will help to put problems into perspective.

Disability and illness

For some older clients, going to bed represents a major and anxiety-provoking challenge. Getting undressed, washed, and dressed in night-clothes can be a daunting, exhausting and time-consuming business. For others, the very thought of night is distressing because it is the time when it is impossible to keep their minds off unpleasant symptoms, such as pain or breathlessness.

How can the care worker help?

Try to achieve the following, as far as possible:

- Make a thorough sleep assessment. In this way, you will have a clearer idea of what the clients expect.
- Continue existing bedtime routines.
- Provide familiar objects – the clients' own clocks, photos, pictures, radios, televisions and so on will provide reassurance.
- Control the general environment, especially temperature, noise and lighting.
- Ensure a balanced programme of day activities.
- Minimise visits to the toilet by encouraging clients:
  - to avoid too much fluid late in the evening (but do not reduce the total amount for the day); and
  - to use the toilet immediately before going to sleep.
- Reduce anxiety by creating a relaxed and good-humoured evening atmosphere in which clients feel free to talk.

- Ensure that medication to help clients sleep is taken according to the doctor's prescription. Always ensure that you record how well clients sleep when taking these drugs, so that senior staff can monitor their effects. If clients are very drowsy during the morning, the doctor may reduce the dose or change the type of medication.

ACTIVITY

Mention has been made of the need for a thorough assessment of sleep. Here are some suggestions for how to go about this.

Information you need from the client:

- How much sleep the client thinks she needs.
- How content she is with her present sleep patterns.
- Whether she thinks these have changed.
- How the client thinks she could improve her sleep.

Information that you need to gather:

- Reports from the night staff about her sleep patterns.

- Assessment of daytime naps – how often and how long.
- Whether reported poor nights are followed by poor days.
- Observation and recording of the client's usual bedtime routine.

Once you have collected sufficient information, discuss the results with your supervisor and colleagues. If necessary, suggest changes to the existing care plan to deal with any problems you have discovered.

4.24 Meeting mental health-care needs: *Managing mood changes*

We all experience a wide range of emotions throughout our lives. To feel sad, happy or anxious is perfectly normal. Most of the time these changes take place in response to alterations in our environment or circumstances. Occasionally, however, they seem to come on without any obvious cause.

Every stage of life has its own particular pleasures and pains, from the anxieties of adolescence, or the joys of parenthood, to the pain of separation and bereavement. Each is a challenge and coping with them helps to make us what we are.

Older clients will have passed through many of these phases: adolescence, marriage, parenthood, work pressures, retirement, bereavement. Through experience they will have developed means of coping. However, the later years often put extra pressure of a person's ability to cope. There are particular reasons for this:

- being an older person means that the end of life is closer;
- physical illnesses or disabilities are more common;
- relationships with loved ones will be changed and may even come to an end through bereavement or illness.

Just being older does not necessarily mean that all these become easier to deal with because of experience. In some cases it does; but there are many older people who find the prospect and experience of old age just as daunting as any younger person might.

It is important for care workers to be aware of the possibility that clients may be reaching the end of their tether. Often the difference between sadness and depression as an illness is merely a matter of degree. Whenever care staff are worried about the mental health of a client, the general practitioner should be asked for assistance. These days many minor mental-health problems are treated in the community with the help of the family doctor together with the local community mental-health team, which includes community nurses and social workers.

The two commonest emotional disorders to keep in mind are depression and anxiety. Both of these can be treated very effectively and so it is vital for care workers to report any concerns they may have.

Depression

Sadness is normal, severe depression is not. How can you tell the difference? The symptoms of depression are physical, psychological and social. Here are the main ones.

Physical symptoms:

- Poor sleep – waking early in the morning is common.
- Feeling lowest in the mornings.
- Poor appetite.
- Constipation.
- Loss of weight.
- Behaviour may slow down, the client being very reluctant to get up and about. Alternatively, the person may become quite agitated and restless while at the same time looking sad and distressed.

Psychological symptoms:

- Feelings of sadness and hopelessness.
- Suicidal feelings – these are often kept hidden but may come out indirectly, for example talking as if there is no future.
- Clients may behave as if they are confused and suffering from dementia. A missed diagnosis of this kind has very serious consequences for the client because depression can be effectively treated and cured, whereas dementia cannot.

Social symptoms:

- Clients may withdraw from other people, preferring to stay on their own and not mix.
- Conversation is often very limited and clients may only respond briefly to questions.
- It may be difficult to make eye contact because they avoid your gaze.

When depression is mild it may be possible to encourage clients to respond to others, perhaps by joining in an appropriate activity. In this way they may feel less depressed and better able to cope with their unpleasant emotions. In other cases this encouragement has no effect at all. Too much 'jollying along' will probably make matters worse. A tactful, sensitive approach is vital towards clients who may be feeling sad and depressed. For clients with more than just a mild depression anti-depressant drugs will probably be prescribed by the general practitioner. Where problems are more severe, clients will be referred by their doctor to a psychiatrist. Always refer clients to their general practitioner at the first sign of depression – early treatment can prevent the condition getting worse.

Anxiety

As with depression, some degree of anxiety is part of our everyday experience. More than this, a little anxiety can actually be helpful, such as before taking examinations or performing in public. Sportsmen and sportswomen often refer to the 'adrenalin pumping' before the start of their events.

The signs that anxiety is getting out of hand and may need special help are as follows:

- Complaints by clients that the anxiety is causing them concern, that they cannot get rid of it by their own efforts.
- Poor concentration.
- Restlessness and irritation with others.
- Difficulty in getting off to sleep.
- Signs of sweating in situations where you would not expect this to occur. The skin feels 'cold and clammy'.
- Rapid breathing. When this is severe it is known as *over-breathing* (or *hyperventilation*) and can lead to dizziness and tingling in the hands and feet.
- Sometimes the hands show a *tremor* – a fine shaking.
- Rapid heartbeats may occur. Clients may complain of experiencing *palpitations*, when they feel their heartbeats as a thumping in the chest. This can be very frightening because they may quite unnecessarily fear heart disease.
- Diarrhoea is common: this can lead clients to worry that they have cancer or some other bowel problem.
- Frequent passing of urine can be very distressing and again cause concern about physical illness.

- Sometimes anxiety is only present in particular situations, such as in crowded places, in the presence of spiders, or in high places. These anxiety conditions are known as *phobias*.

This list shows how anxiety can cause symptoms that mimic physical disease. However, be careful not to jump to the conclusion that anxiety is causing physical symptoms. It might be, but physical illness must be ruled out first.

If the client is seriously anxious, the general practitioner will refer the client to the psychiatrist and community mental health-care team. They will be able to help the client cope with his or her anxieties, perhaps through learning special techniques of anxiety management, like relaxation therapy. Medication is sometimes used, but normally for only a short period because of the dangers of dependency.

ACTIVITY

1 Look at the list of symptoms of depression. How many clients do you know who have one or more of these?

Probably you will discover quite a few. Remember that one or two symptoms are never enough to make a diagnosis of a mental illness. It is the whole picture that is most important.

2 Do you think you have some clients at high risk of depression? Why do you think this? What do you feel you could do to lower this risk?

3 Do you recognise anxiety and depression as emotions that you have had to deal with yourself? If so, what have you learned from your own experiences that would help you to care better for clients in a similar position?

4.25   Meeting mental health-care needs: *Helping confused clients*

There are many reasons why older people become confused. Often there is an organic cause – that is, there is interference with the proper functioning of the brain cells. Many conditions can bring this about. If the underlying cause is treated quickly, confusion can frequently be cured. It follows that, like depression, it is an illness that needs to be recognised early so that medical help can be sought as soon as possible.

What is confusion?

In everyday language, 'confusion' is used to describe the state of someone who is bewildered or whose behaviour is muddled. This is also true of the older client who is confused; but care workers need to know how to recognise it more precisely. The main features of confusion are these:

- The problem usually comes on quite quickly, in the space of a day or two.
- The level of mental confusion varies quite a bit. Often it is at its worst in the evening, as night begins to fall. In fact, anything that makes the environment less clear and predictable will cause greater confusion.
- Emotionally, confused clients switch rapidly from one extreme to the other – from apparent contentment one minute to irritation and anger the next.
- Drowsiness is common but this also varies a good deal throughout the day.
- Concentration is very poor and the client's mind wanders easily.
- Clients frequently misunderstand what is going on around them. They may misidentify people or misinterpret their actions. They often look frightened and bewildered. Sometimes clients falsely believe that they are about to be harmed or are in some other kind of serious danger.
- They may experience things that are not really there. Such experiences are called *hallucinations* and can affect any of the senses. Voices or sounds may be heard, or clients may see strange objects, animals or people.
- Most clients look physically unwell. Exactly how they will be suffering depends on the particular cause – for example sweating due to high temperature or breathlessness due to heart failure.

Causes of confusion

- *Infections* Common examples are chest infections (for example, long-standing bronchitis which may lead to pneumonia) and urinary infections.
- *Heart failure* This causes less oxygen to reach the brain. The problem will be made worse if the client already has hardened and narrowed arteries.
- *Poor diet (malnutrition)* Confusion is especially likely to follow if clients have had insufficient vitamins.
- *Too little to drink (dehydration)* This will be worse if the client is also losing fluid through diarrhoea or vomiting.
- *Hypothermia* This is described in section 4.22.

- *Pain and discomfort* Severe pain and long-standing discomfort (for example, constipation).
- *Head injury* This may result from a fall.
- *Drugs* There are a large number of prescribed drugs that may cause confusion. With age the body becomes less able to break down drugs and so toxic effects are more likely to occur. Examples are steroids (used for such conditions as asthma and some forms of arthritis), sleeping tablets and drugs used to lower blood pressure.
- *Other illnesses* Many diseases can cause confusion, especially in vulnerable older clients. Examples are failure of the liver and kidneys, and diabetes.
- *Psychological causes* Major stresses also can cause confusion, such as the death of a loved one or a sudden change of circumstances (for example, a move into residential care).

Managing confusion

The first aim must be to treat the cause, so the sooner medical advice is sought the better. In addition to this, the priorities should be these:

Maintain a safe environment

Observe confused clients closely at all times – it is very easy for their confused behaviour to put them at considerable physical risk. Encourage clients to move away from areas of potential danger, such as the kitchen or bathroom. Instead, try to encourage them to take an interest in a simple, safe activity, such as helping you to make a bed. Because confused clients have poor concentration and are easily distracted, you may find it fairly easy to move their attention away from unsafe situations. Ideally, they should be cared for one-to-one in these circumstances.

Reassure the client by being calm and unhurried

This can be most difficult because confused behaviour can be extremely demanding and frustrating for the care worker. It is important for you to tell your supervisor if you are getting stressed: someone else should be able to relieve you for a while. If all care workers behave in this way, they can support one another by ensuring that no one person has to deal with a confused client for too long a period.

Encourage proper rest

The normal day/night cycle is broken when clients are confused – they may get up in the middle of the night, thinking it is morning. The normal pattern should be restored as soon as possible by gently reminding clients what time of day it is and what they are expected to do.

Maintain good nourishment

Encourage an adequate level of fluid intake and a balanced diet, given in a form that clients can manage. With very confused clients, liquid supplements may be essential. Even in this form, you may find it difficult to persuade clients to take sufficient. The key is patience and gentle persistence. Never show irritation to clients even if you are feeling rather frustrated – it can be guaranteed to make matters worse.

Observe carefully how often clients are going to the toilet

If little urine is passed, this may indicate that dehydration is occurring due to insufficient fluid intake. Constipation may also occur because of a change in diet or because regular patterns have been broken by the mental confusion. Both dehydration and constipation may cause the confusion to worsen, so good observation is essential. Tell your supervisor if you have any concerns about a confused client.

Ensure that general physical care is not neglected

It is important to ensure proper hygiene, cleanliness and mouth care. When confused, clients are rarely able to meet many of their basic needs and you have an important duty to see that these aspects of care are carried out with the dignity of the client in mind.

ACTIVITY

1 You might find it difficult to understand what clients feel when they are suffering from confusion. Try to remember an occasion when you found yourself in a place that was new to you. It might have been a strange hotel, railway station or airport. In these situations, we often feel a slight panic and sense of disorientation, especially if we are on our own and there are no friendly faces to help us out. Imagine the sort of person you would most have liked to come to your rescue.

- What sort of qualities would he or she have had?
- What types of behaviours would have been most reassuring to you?

2 Discuss this with your supervisor and colleagues. Are there any lessons here for the care of the confused client?

4.26 Meeting mental health-care needs: *Challenging dementia* (1)

Understanding dementia

Dementia is one of the most distressing and serious illnesses of old age. It changes personalities and relationships; damages the quality of life for the person affected and all those around; and creates great social isolation and loneliness.

In fact it comprises several different illnesses, but these all cause very similar problems for the sufferer, relatives and care workers. The most usual type of dementia is known as Alzheimer's disease. Some of the normal changes of old age are easily confused with the symptoms of dementia. Always keep in mind, however, that dementia is an *illness*, not just another name for the unwanted effects of old age. These are the main symptoms.

Poor short-term memory

Clients find it hard to remember recent events, such as what they had for their last meal, but may be able to recall episodes from their childhood.

Loss of contact with reality

Clients begin to lose their grip on reality. They may feel frightened and insecure because they may not know where they are, who they or others are, or what the time of day is. Technically, these changes are known respectively as *disorientation in place*, *disorientation in person* and *disorientation in time*. Not knowing the time of day can lead to numerous problems. Confused people often get up at midnight but behave as if it was midday.

Although in the early stages they know that something is wrong, as time goes by this insight is lost. Normal rational conversation eventually becomes impossible.

Changes in behaviour

Many people with dementia become quite agitated and restless. Their immediate world has become a place of uncertainty and bewilderment. There is no longer an anchor in reality to provide security.

Coping with life's varied demands becomes increasingly difficult. Sometimes things reach such a pitch that the client does not know how to handle the situation at all. He or she may then refuse to cooperate, show anger towards those around or become very emotional and weepy. This is called a *catastrophe reaction*. The problem may seem to be quite trivial, such as how to get dressed, but the challenge is just too much. For someone who is confused, even such an apparently simple act is a massive mountain to climb.

Other behaviour changes that can be most distressing are due to what is known as *disinhibition* – that is, the normal brakes on our everyday behaviour are removed. For much of our lives we have to conform to various social rules, such as being polite to strangers, dressing appropriately, and not exposing our sexual organs, or masturbating, in public. Some clients with dementia will behave in ways that break these rules.

Communication problems

Just as actions are made more difficult by dementia, so is speech. Clients with very severe dementia are often unable to communicate in the ordinary sense of the word. Their speech is incoherent and without apparent meaning. At an earlier stage, though, communication is distorted but not interrupted altogether. The names of common objects may be forgotten but clients will make efforts to get the message across using other descriptions. For example, the word 'knife' might not be remembered. Instead a client may speak of 'cutting ... thing to slice'. She may well also use hand movements to illustrate what she is trying to say.

Dealing with problems

The changes that dementia brings about create many problems for clients and relatives. This section and the next look at several of the most difficult and how care workers can help.

Wandering

One of the greatest worries for care workers and relatives alike is that the client will wander off and come to harm. These worries are justified because a number of lives are lost in this way every year, mainly during the winter.

Why do clients wander?

- Memory losses and disorientation may cause them to be unaware of where they are, who they are, or what the time of day or year might be. Each is sufficient to encourage wandering.
- Clients may be looking for a lost person or place. This is often connected to a strong sense of loss and bereavement.
- They may be frightened and anxious. Wandering might then be a way of searching for greater security.
- Clients who are in pain and discomfort may not be able to communicate this through words. Wandering may be a means of expressing this distress.
- In care settings where there are few planned activities, wandering may be the clients' response to boredom, lack of stimulation or lack of exercise.

Care of clients who wander

Taking risks

The biggest dilemma is often how to allow clients as much freedom as possible while at the same time reducing risks and dangers. Managing risks is one of the critical areas for all care workers. It should be a team responsibility. Everyone concerned with the care of clients needs to be involved. Care workers, their supervisors, relatives and relevant professionals should all be included in assessing the level of risk and in coming to decisions about the best course of action. If everyone is satisfied that their point of view has been considered, there will be far fewer problems later.

Assessment

The objective should be to prevent the problem by removing the reasons for wandering. A thorough assessment of clients' needs should be the basis for the general plan of care.

If wandering occurs, reassessment will be necessary to try to discover the reasons why. Does it occur at night, in the day, or day and night? Is it provoked by a particular situation? Occasionally a clear reason can be found, for example pain or discomfort, and then the solution is usually to remove the cause. Clients may also start to wander following a change of environment. More often than not the wandering will reduce as the clients get used to the new environment. Unfortunately, straightforward solutions are rather uncommon. In most cases, care workers are in the position of having to deal with the problem without any detailed understanding of the cause.

What can be done in these circumstances? A plan of care designed to keep the clients fit, active and involved will reduce the likelihood of wandering. It is also important to note any changes in clients' behaviours, such as an increase in general restlessness.

Identification

Clients who are prone to wander need to have effective identification on them. Identity bracelets can be used which show name, address and telephone number. These can be quite attractive. Other methods, such as encouraging clients to carry identification in pockets and bags, are much less reliable. Clients might lose the identification; and people finding a lost client will often be understandably reluctant to search through the belongings of a total stranger to find some identification.

Neighbours

It is a good idea to let neighbours know about the possibility of clients wandering. Enlisting their help will reduce the risk of clients wandering too far away. By doing this we are also recognising the needs of the neighbours, most of whom would prefer to have clear guidance on action they can take.

Getting a client back

If a vulnerable client tries to leave, care workers should never use force to restrain the person. Try talking gently and perhaps introduce a new subject. Involve another care worker or another client to distract the potential wanderer. This simple suggestion will often work, but not always. If the client is determined to leave, don't try confrontation but walk out together and through persuasion, and perhaps a hand on the arm, gradually manoeuvre the person back to safety. A round trip back home will quite often be enough to satisfy a client's wanderlust.

However anxious you may feel, never show any frustration or anger. It will only make matters much worse. Get rid of any emotions with colleagues later. There are always lessons to be learned when a client either tries to wander away or has to be brought back. Together with your supervisor, you should try to make positive use of these experiences by finding better ways of dealing with future problems.

ACTIVITY

Imagine what it must be like to have a poor recent memory. You will be talking to someone, telling them a story perhaps, yet within two minutes you will have forgotten completely what it was you just said.

As a care worker, how are you going to deal with situations like this?

ACTIVITY

1 Select one or two clients you know who suffer from dementia. Observe their behaviour at different times of the day and in different situations. Are there links between the clients' behaviours and the circumstances they find themselves in? For example is getting up in the morning more difficult than sitting down and eating a meal? Are there behaviour changes that seem to depend on the time of day?

2 Discuss this with colleagues and your supervisor. What can you do to improve care for these clients?

This first-hand account describes the feelings of a relative – a social services manager – who spent a weekend caring for his father, who suffers from dementia.

I waved goodbye and closed the door. The staff had taken over, gently leading my father to his meal. He had already forgotten me. I got in the car and drove home as quickly as I could, longing for uninterrupted normality. It had been an exhausting weekend.

My father is 83 and suffers from senile dementia. It had been creeping along insidiously in the 10 years since my mother had died. He would forget to turn off the gas, would not eat properly, would suddenly go out in the middle of the night, knocking up the neighbours about some urgent problem to do with the job he'd left over 15 years ago.

Despite extra home care and meals on wheels, despite more frequent visits from his family and neighbours, in the end it was obvious he could not cope any more, and with some difficulty we eventually found him a specialist local authority home for elderly mentally infirm people.

He has the privacy of his own room, good and caring staff, and we visit as often as we can. Nevertheless, we wanted him to come and stay with us like he used to before he became senile. Hence the weekend, and hence my exhaustion.

What did I learn from it? First the sheer strain of physical care. My father could not be left alone at all. He had to be helped with everything – washing, feeding, dressing and toileting. I am physically fit, but the constancy was draining – even more so because it was so hard to get rest. I slept in the same room, listening like a cat to his wheezing, putting him back to bed when he wanted to wander, changing his incontinence pads if I got up in time, or the sheets if I did not.

Senility is also another land, and the people who live there are different. However contented they may be, there is no short-term memory – only the immediate present, the objects and faces in front of their eyes, and then the distant past. My father would often go back there – but not to reminisce, rather to live.

He would genuinely think he was a little boy, or just starting work. It is eerie to see someone look outward, through you, into his inward world. Sometimes there would be flickers of personality traits that had been there all his life.

Very occasionally the whole person would visit us from this strange land – the sun would peep through the clouds and there would be brief lucid conversations, but then the clouds would close over again. It was a very disturbing and disorienting to experience over a protracted period. . . .

The weekend also rekindled my anger; the reminder that improvement will not spontaneously happen. It needs a fire in the belly which is a vital antidote to the burnt out defensiveness or glib management-speak that too often slides away from appropriate confrontation and political assertiveness. . . .

So as I waved goodbye and closed the door on him, then, even in his senility, my father still opened doors for me.

(This extract is reproduced with the kind permission of *Care Weekly*.)

4.27 Meeting mental health-care needs: *Challenging dementia* (2)

Undressing

It is not uncommon for people with dementia to start undressing in totally inappropriate places, such as in the sitting room in front of strangers. This is always very disturbing and embarrassing for relatives and visitors. Care workers, too, find the problem distressing. Like wandering, the reasons for the behaviour are often obscure.

- Disorientation is an obvious cause. Clients who are muddled about the time of day or where they are may think it is the right time and place to get undressed.
- Discomfort should be considered. Are clothes uncomfortable? Are they appropriate for the environment? Perhaps the person is too hot. This might indicate that the client is running a temperature due to infection.
- Undressing is also a means of getting attention, especially when the client's abilities to communicate have been damaged by dementia. For some clients, pain or perhaps the need to go to the toilet could be at the root of the problem.

The first priority in managing clients who behave in this way is assessment – for example, does the client give any explanation? Is there a pattern to the behaviour, such as time of day, or one place rather than another?

You need to be able to deal with the client's behaviour with great tact. Having to intervene when an older person has just taken her dress off 'in public' can be extremely awkward. If relatives are present at the same time, the situation is even more difficult. You should adopt a tactful, matter-of-fact approach. Sometimes it helps to be a little lighthearted about the situation, but this must be done with sensitivity.

It is important to give relatives a chance to express their shock and distress, and for them to try to understand something of why their loved one may behave in this way. Educating relatives about dementia needs to include explanations of this kind. The problem is always a considerable one but will be particularly traumatic in groups whose culture traditionally involves keeping the body covered to a large extent.

Sexual behaviour

The loss of control that is seen in dementia sometimes leads clients to express sexual behaviour openly. Masturbation in public is probably the most difficult to deal with. Your approach should be along the lines recommended for coping with undressing. Being able to obtain sexual satisfaction through masturbation is the right of anyone, of course: you should be careful not to reproach clients for the behaviour. They should not be made to feel guilty about what is a perfectly normal act. The challenge is to avoid it occurring in a publicly humiliating way.

Another form of sexual behaviour that can cause difficulty is where a client touches staff, visitors or other clients in a sexually provocative way. Again, a tactful intervention is required. Exactly how to respond in any particular instance depends very much on your knowledge of the client's personality and general behaviour. You may find this especially hard to cope with at first. Because of this, it is essential for you to discuss this with your supervisor as soon as possible after the event.

Aggression

A very natural response to aggression is to be aggressive back – to retaliate, verbally or physically. This is one of the reasons why you need to think carefully about the circumstances that bring about aggression and how you should react. Emotions need to be kept under control during aggressive incidents.

Aggression in older clients is usually due to one of several factors:

- *Fear* – for example, the client may believe that you are an intruder.
- *Failure to cope* – frustration is one of the main causes of aggression and clients may be very aware of how much more competent they were when younger.
- *Humiliation* – having to accept help from strangers can be a devastating experience and one reaction is to turn against those carrying out the tasks.
- *Confrontation* – for example, if a care worker deals with wandering in an abrupt and authoritarian manner.
- *Pain and discomfort* – confused clients may hit out if they are suffering physically, for example because of constipation.

Knowing clients well is the key to preventing aggression. Early signs can be detected and action taken before things get worse. Tension and anxiety, restlessness, wandering, frustration and irritability – all are signs that the client may be reaching boiling point. However, some verbal aggression is perfectly normal, even necessary, and can help to defuse situations that otherwise might lead to physical violence.

Dealing with aggression

- Stay as calm as you can. Don't retaliate.
- If you have been attacked physically, you have the right to defend yourself but only by using the amount of force necessary to prevent further harm to yourself.
- Don't confront – it is likely to provoke further aggression.
- It might help to move away from the situation; in any case, try not to crowd the client. If you do, this could be seen as threatening.
- If some physical restraint is necessary, never do this on your own. Get help from colleagues and follow the local procedures under the supervision of the senior person on duty. Try to keep the aggressive person away from other clients, to prevent any harm to them.
- Always make sure that the incident is reported and recorded in detail as soon as possible. There may well be an investigation into exactly what happened.
- Aggressive incidents should be used as learning experiences for everyone. Aggression is often unpredictable and your responses can never be controlled completely. It can take some time for you to recover from an unexpected outburst of aggression. You may feel unnecessarily guilty because you didn't manage to prevent it. Or it may leave you feeling confused and let down by the client. Whatever the reaction, it is important for everyone to have the chance afterwards to talk over how they felt at the time and subsequently.

ACTIVITY

Talk to your supervisor about the situations covered in this section. What strategies could you devise to prevent these problems occurring? Find out whether there are any written policies available in your work setting – for example, a policy on the use of physical restraint to deal with a violent client.

Reading on . . .

★ The Alzheimer's Disease Society publishes very useful *Information Sheets* and *Advice Sheets*. Details from The Alzheimer's Disease Society, 158–160 Balham High Road, London SW12 9BN (081–67 6557/8/9/0).

★ Marilyn Harvey's book *Who Confused?* (PEPAR Publications 1990) is a mine of practical information and advice.

★ A comprehensive account of caring at home for confused old people is *The 36-Hour Day*, published in 1985 by Edward Arnold in conjunction with Age Concern. Originally an American publication, it has been adapted for the British market. The authors, Nancy Mace and Peter Rabins, describe the problems of caring for a person suffering from dementia.

4.28 Meeting spiritual needs

What are spiritual needs?

As earlier sections have shown, care workers should be prepared to assess clients' spiritual needs. For many clients, spiritual needs are the same as religious needs: that is, they express their spiritual beliefs through membership of an organised religion. Other clients, however, choose not to belong to any particular religion. They will still have spiritual needs but they choose to deal with them on a more personal, individual level.

Spiritual needs are special. They are abstract rather than concrete: they do not present themselves directly as physical problems with physical solutions. They may be hard to recognise, both for the care worker and for the client. However, they are just as important for the clients as any of the more obvious physical needs. If spiritual needs are not met, clients can become dispirited, depressed and dissatisfied with their lives. They will not be able to enjoy life as they would wish, nor fight illness so effectively.

With increasing age clients often pay more attention to spiritual matters. There are good reasons for this – for example:

- There is an awareness that the body will not last for ever, that death is closer. Many want to feel peace of mind in their final years.
- Having passed through those stages of life that are full of change and activity – jobs, marriage, children and so on – clients may ask 'What else is left?'
- Many older clients will wish to try to make sense of their lives, to find a way of understanding their place in the order of things.
- Older clients may wish to renew their religious practices. They may feel that they have neglected them when younger, perhaps due to other more immediate responsibilities.

These spiritual questions are just as relevant whether clients are Christian, Muslim, Hindu, Jewish .. or without any formal belief at all.

How can care workers help?

Respect individual beliefs

Show respect towards individual beliefs through your general attitudes in all aspects of your behaviour. Try to develop a genuine interest in the beliefs and religions of others. But understand also your own beliefs and practices, and how these might clash with those of clients. This is easy to write but sometimes hard to put into practice. You can be willing to learn without having to agree.

Nevertheless, there are times when you may find the beliefs of some clients worrying. For example, because of their own beliefs some Christians find it quite distressing when others worship physical images of their god or gods. If tensions do arise, talk about these concerns with your supervisor. Care workers should not seek to impose their beliefs on clients in any way, either directly by challenging them or indirectly by failing to support the clients' attempts to practise their beliefs.

Recognise the range of beliefs

Try to understand the range of spiritual and religious beliefs and practices of the clients in your care setting. British society is made up of a wide range of cultures and people from different ethnic backgrounds. The table on page 139 shows how diverse customs can be.

Keep in mind that most religions occur in a great many varieties. Not all Christians will share every belief; neither will all Muslims. So be careful not to develop stereotyped views of particular religious groups. Always check beliefs and practices directly with individual clients.

Allow clients plenty of time to talk about their beliefs and philosophies. It will be a minority of clients, perhaps, who start to talk about this topic in an explicit way. Most will give you a clue to their feelings on this through other subjects of conversation, such as their hopes and expectations, how they see their earlier experiences, and so on.

Where clients are unable to explain fully their spiritual or religious needs, try to gain as much information as you can from relatives or friends so that you may still supply support.

Encourage religious observances

Provide clients with access to the materials and circumstances they need to carry out their religious practices. For some, this will mean finding the correct place for certain holy objects. Sikhs, for example, require that nothing should be placed on top of their holy book – the Guru Grant Sahib. For others, such as Muslims, it might mean adapting the routine to allow ritual prayers to be said, and providing the right environment for this – for example, by moving the bed so that the client can face in the right direction.

Clients who don't already have contact with others of similar faith can be helped to make these links. These may include lay people and also priests or ministers, from a local religious group.

Ensure that you know where to contact key people when needed. The telephone numbers and addresses of ministers of religions who can be contacted should be kept easily accessible.

Keep a calendar of religious events so that festivals can be recognised and celebrated. Exactly how this is achieved will depend on the care setting and the numbers of clients sharing particular beliefs.

ACTIVITY

1 Dealing with clients' spiritual needs is always a demanding aspect of care for older people. You should spend some time thinking about the following questions.

- How would you describe your own spiritual needs?
- How do you go about meeting these needs?
- From your experience, how well do you think clients' spiritual needs are met?
- What actions could you take to improve the quality of this aspect of care?

2 Now discuss these improvements with your supervisor, and perhaps contact local religious leaders.

Reading on . . .

★ It is impossible to do justice to this topic in only a few pages. There are many excellent general introductions to different religions available from public libraries.

★ The National Extension College publishes several very useful books on caring for clients from different ethnic minority religions. The address is given on page 149.

★ Another helpful publication dealing specifically with older clients is *Multicultural Health Care and Rehabilitation of Older People*, edited by Amanda Squires and published by Edward Arnold (with Age Concern) in 1991.

DIFFERENT RELIGIOUS PRACTICES

Buddhism

- *Founder* Buddha.
- *God's name* None.
- *Holy books* Tripitaka, Pali Canon, Dhammapada.
- *Main countries* Sri Lanka, Japan, Thailand, Burma.
- *Main festivals* Vesakha (May); Kathina (October); Dhanima (Chakha day).
- *Common beliefs/practices* Reincarnation; no alcohol; the Sangha (order of monks – 'bhikkhus').

Islam

- *Founder* Mohammed.
- *God's name* Allah.
- *Holy book* Qur'an.
- *Main countries* Saudi Arabia, Iran, Pakistan.
- *Main festivals* Ramadan (August/September).
- *Common beliefs/practices* No pork is eaten or alcohol drunk; male circumcision.

Christianity

- *Founder* Jesus Christ.
- *God's name* God.
- *Holy book* The Bible.
- *Main countries* Britain, France, Italy, USA.
- *Main festivals* Christmas; Easter.
- *Common beliefs/practices* Christening; holy communion; confession.

Judaism

- *Founder* Moses.
- *God's name* Yahwah.
- *Holy book* Torah.
- *Main countries* Israel, Britain, USA.
- *Main festivals* Rosh Hashanah (New Year); Passover (March or April); Yom Kippur (September or October).
- *Common beliefs/practices* Male circumcision; no pork or shellfish are eaten; fasting on Yom Kippur.

Hinduism

- *Founder* No single person.
- *God's name* Many, including Krishna, Shiva, Kali.
- *Holy book* Bhagavad Gita (part of the Mahabharata).
- *Main countries* India.
- *Main festivals* Diwali (October or November); Holi (February or March).
- *Common beliefs/practices* Cremation; reincarnation; no meat is eaten.

Sikhism

- *Founder* Nanak.
- *God's name* Sat Nam.
- *Holy book* Guru Grant Sahib.
- *Main countries* India (Punjab).
- *Main festivals* Baisakhi (April); Diwali (October or November).
- *Common beliefs/practices* Five signs: wrist bangle; uncut hair and beard; comb; symbolic dagger; undershorts.

4.29 Loss, bereavement and growth: *Everyone's experience*

Loss is a universal experience. We have to come to terms with it from our very earliest days. For most people, this understanding takes place gradually through a series of experiences beginning in childhood. Although they are unwelcome and often distressing we learn to cope with them: the loss of friends, pets or familiar surroundings, for instance.

Older people usually will have gone through many of these experiences – in some cases, and most profoundly, the loss of a partner. Because of this you might think that clients are well prepared for losses to come, for the later years inevitably bring with them the realisation that things cannot stay the same as they were. But the ultimate loss – our own death – can never truly be prepared for. We can accept its inevitability in an intellectual sense, that is we know we shall die one day, because we are only human. But can we ever accept it emotionally?

It is also true, however, that the experience of surviving a major loss can bring benefits to the individual. The personality may become richer and wiser, and this growth can often be put to good use in helping others survive similar circumstances. You can learn a great deal from listening carefully to your clients' experiences of loss. The fact that they may have coped with severe hardship and tragedy, yet survived, can be a starting point for greater self-understanding.

The thought of death – our own or others' – often stimulates two quite different emotions: fascination and fear. Fascination, because of the mystery of death. Is there life after death? Is death like going to sleep? Fear, because we don't know how we will die. Will dying be painful? Will I die in an accident? Will I die in my sleep? 'I don't fear death but I do fear dying' is a common statement.

Reactions to loss

More than twenty years ago, Dr Elizabeth Kübler-Ross described five stages that dying people pass through in reacting to their own impending death. Knowledge of these stages is useful in understanding more about how clients feel and react. But it isn't just the dying person who has to deal with this emotional turmoil. It is relatives and friends too. And staff as well, especially where caring relationships between clients and care workers have become close.

The five stages are these.

Stage 1 Denial

'No, not me!' '*I'm* not dying.'

Sometimes the client and relatives will behave as if nothing has changed. The thought of imminent death is simply too horrific to be accepted. You should not try to challenge this attitude but should allow clients to take their own time, showing patience and acceptance.

Stage 2 Anger

'Why *me*!'

The anger and aggression are usually verbal, but are nonetheless distressing for relatives and staff. However, this reaction may stiffen the

ACTIVITY

This topic is difficult and uncomfortable because we are dealing with what is perhaps the most basic of human fears. Nevertheless, from time to time, it is important to face your own feelings about loss and death. In this way, you may become more sensitive to the fears and anxieties of the clients in your care.

There are a number of questions here that you should consider. Do this on your own if you wish. But it can also be valuable to discuss your personal reactions with others. If you have undergone a recent bereavement yourself, it may not be helpful to you to start the exercise at this stage: you must be the judge of this.

- Do you think about your own death? How often?
- Has your thinking on this changed as you have grown older?
- Think about one particular loss that you have experienced. It does not have to be connected with death. It might be the loss of a job, for example. How far do you think Kübler-Ross's ideas could be applied to that experience?

ACTIVITY

Discuss with your supervisor your thoughts about bereavement and loss. As a result, can you think of ways to improve the care of clients?

clients' determination to get the most out of the life that is left. You should try to see the value in this response and help relatives to cope.

Stage 3 Bargaining

'If I agree to ——, don't let me die, God.' 'Let me live until I have seen my grandchild born.'

You must be prepared to help clients when it becomes apparent that the 'bargain' is not going to work. The right balance is hard to achieve. Clients have every right to retain hope until the last, and no one can say absolutely that another person is going to die at any particular time. So it is important to be guided by the client's own attitude and awareness of the situation.

Stage 4 Depression

'Oh no, it *is* me . . . I'm going to die.'

To react with depression at some stage is to be normal. It is rational because dying people are about to lose everything that means anything to them. Trying to discourage feelings of depression is unlikely to help in the long run. Nevertheless, when clients begin to express more positive emotions, perhaps looking back proudly on past achievements, you should encourage this.

Stage 5 Acceptance

'I accept that I am dying, and I am ready.'

Older clients will sometimes say that they feel ready to die, like a tired person who is longing to go to sleep. This should not be seen as a negative or unwanted feeling. It can be a period of happiness and contentment. If clients and relatives both understand the situation, communication can be open and honest. However, you should be aware that there is no guarantee that clients will remain in this state of mind all the time. Other reactions, such as anger and depression, are also likely to be seen again from time to time. You should anticipate this.

Respecting individuality

However useful Dr Kübler-Ross's ideas are, remember that all individuals are different. Feelings are complex and changeable and will not conform simply to anybody's theory. We each have our own unique way of coping with death and dying. Some older people are more worried about the death of their partner than they are about their own – a man may say, 'I hope she goes first', hoping that he will be able to look after her. Other clients will stay angry with the thought of death and appear not to accept it – this is their right, their way of coping.

Try to use the ideas here to understand better the individual client. In this way, the care you offer will be more sensitive.

4.30 Loss, bereavement and growth: *The dying person*

Caring for people who are close to death is, for most care workers, the greatest challenge of their professional lives. Ideally, each client should have had the opportunity to talk about his or her own attitudes to death, if she or he wishes, before the final stages. This is not always possible, however. Some clients do not wish, or cannot bring themselves, to speak about it. In other circumstances, clients may have been admitted into residential care only recently and have had no chance to develop the kinds of relationships in which such conversations become possible. So, as a care worker, you have to be prepared for many different sets of circumstances.

Spiritual help

There are few older people who have not at some point thought about their own mortality. When death is imminent, this is even more pressing. For some there will be comfort in membership of an organised religion. Ministers may need to be contacted where this has not been done already by relatives or friends.

But it is not just a question of organisation. The client needs the opportunity to talk about these urgent questions when they arise. This can present problems for care workers who sometimes find it difficult to deal with clients at this stage in their lives. Everyone, however experienced, finds this disturbing. However, it is something which, if faced with courage and compassion, will lead to a deeper understanding of the client and of the process of dying. Those caring for clients may sometimes join in a conspiracy of silence. It is sometimes more comfortable for both clients and staff to talk about the weather or routine events in the unit. When the time is right, however, clients should be encouraged to talk freely about their feelings. They may wish to clear up misunderstandings with relatives or friends, or to express feelings that may not have been dealt with earlier. There may also be practical details to be handled – wills, for example. Give clients every opportunity to discuss their wishes regarding making a will. Involve your supervisor at an early stage so that independent legal advice and help can be obtained as soon as possible.

Communication problems

Clients who have communication difficulties will need extra help. If speech is difficult – due to a stroke, for example – other means will have to be used. Relatives or a minister may read passages from religious texts, if the client wishes; religious objects can be put within sight; and appropriate music might be used. Where clients are hampered in their communication by confusion and disorientation, the challenges are greater still. Music the client likes can be calming and bring back feelings of spiritual comfort. Similarly, religious pictures and statuettes might be positioned within range of the client.

With someone who is rather confused, it can be helpful to arrange to be with the client at specific times – this will ensure that he or she is not neglected. By using touch to establish contact and then bringing particular objects or sounds to the attention of the client, you may be able to help the client create a link with earlier memories and beliefs. You should discuss this with the client's minister or spiritual leader.

Clients who are socially or culturally isolated will need particular assistance. Where the client is from a particular ethnic culture, try to establish contact with members of the relevant community. More can then be learnt about his or her particular needs and expectations, which will allow you to provide care that is more relevant and sensitive.

Religious rituals

Not all clients have a strong religious faith and yet all have spiritual needs. Some may have been part of an organised religious community at an earlier period in their lives but have since lost touch. Every religion has its own approach to the needs of the dying. You should try to ensure that you know how to meet these needs for all your clients, not just those who are close to death.

Many faiths expect a minister to be called to attend to perform holy rites. These practices will vary considerably and you should be prepared to help if requested. Family or priests may wish to read passages from the holy book or to say prayers. Some may want to sing hymns. Every effort should be made to provide privacy for these needs to be met.

After death, there will again be different requirements for last offices. Many religions prefer the body to be touched only by others of the same faith. Non-believers may have to wear disposable gloves. Always make every effort to find out the wishes of relatives in this respect.

Physical care

The detailed physical care of dying clients is beyond the scope of this book. Nevertheless it is important for you to appreciate some of the common symptoms that clients may experience.

- *Pain* Pain control is now achievable and much better understood; pain killers, administered according to a carefully worked out schedule, can prevent pain.

- *Incontinence* This is very upsetting to the client. In the final stages the insertion of a catheter into the bladder can relieve much distress.

- *Difficulty in breathing* Attention to the client's position in bed can help, as will proper room ventilation. Drugs may be prescribed.

- *Bedsores* Regular gentle turning will help, if this is possible. Equipment to relieve the pressure should be used too.

- *Constipation* An appropriate diet will assist with preventing this problem. Laxative drugs may also be necessary.

- *Nausea and vomiting* Small, easily digested and attractive meals should be offered. Proper care of the mouth and teeth will also help. Drugs may be prescribed.

ACTIVITY

If you have had experience of caring for a dying client, apply this experience as you think about the following questions. (If not, try imagining how it would be. This is a very helpful way of preparing yourself for this difficult experience.) Discuss your responses with colleagues and your supervisor.

- How well do you think you coped?
- What were the most difficult aspects – for example, the physical or the psychological care? Can these be separated anyway?
- How did you find communicating with the client? Was it easy or difficult?
- How did you feel after the client's death?
- What did you learn from this experience that could improve how you care for clients in the future?

4.31 Loss, bereavement and growth: *Caring for relatives and staff*

The reactions experienced by the client who is dying may also be shared by relatives and, to a lesser extent, care workers. The care offered to relatives before and immediately after the person's death can be important in helping them to adjust to the new situation and in preventing later psychological problems. Remember that some clients become bereaved while they are in care and they will need sensitive support to help them cope with this. Staff also need to be looked after at these times.

Caring for the relatives

The living have to face their distress after the client's death. This has to be kept in mind by care workers, as does the knowledge that, however depressed and miserable the bereaved person is at the time, most people do successfully come to terms with the loss. However, it can take a considerable time.

The various stages that relatives go through in this process can bring out a wide range of emotions. No one can predict their own reactions at the death of a loved one. Often unexpected and unwanted surges of emotion, such as guilt, overwhelm the person. Sometimes this is expressed as irritation or anger towards care workers. Bereavement often recalls long-forgotten aspects of our relationship with the dead person – and the bereaved person is more prone to react in unfamiliar ways.

The impact on care workers will depend on many factors, including whether the relatives were regular visitors and had developed a good relationship with care staff in the preceding weeks and months. The most difficult situations to deal with are often those in which the relationship between the client and relatives has been rather strained, with little in the way of overt affection. In these situations, death prevents the bereaved relatives putting things right. Guilt, frustration and anger can result. You should do your best to show your understanding of this process by the way in which you deal with the negative emotions expressed by some relatives. Offer time and support to the relatives to allow them to express their feelings.

Remember that your clients may also be bereaved while in care. In these cases, you must be especially careful to show the client the same sensitivity and regard that you would a bereaved relative who is not a client already. Clients who are bereaved in these circumstances may be very upset, frustrated and guilty that they are unable to take responsibility for arranging funeral details, contacting relatives and so on. Try to ensure that a client in this situation is involved as much as possible, by encouraging the relatives to discuss with the client what is being arranged.

Death also gives rise to practical problems for the relatives. Not all will know the procedures that have to be followed and it is important that you can offer advice on this. There will also be the difficult but necessary matter of dealing with the dead client's belongings. You will have to guide relatives through these administrative requirements in a competent yet caring way. It is not uncommon for bereaved people to feel helpless and at a loss. By handling matters with kindness and confidence, you can help to make the bereaved person's tasks a little easier to bear.

Different cultural groups need to mourn in their own particular ways – you should be aware of this and show understanding. In some cultures it is expected that the bereaved will display their feelings of grief very publicly. This contrasts with present-day British culture where grief is often seen as a private and individual affair with little communal support being offered.

Caring for staff

The death of a client affects everyone connected with that person. Even in situations where death is a likely event, as of course it is when caring for older people, care workers will feel the impact. Although everyone will handle the stresses in their own individual way, thought should be given to how mutual support can be provided. How can this be achieved?

Support groups

Regular meetings of staff will allow sharing of feelings and anxieties. Where staff have to deal with dying clients regularly, the need for such a group is very obvious. In other settings they could be used as and when necessary. The advantage of participating in a support group is that it can prevent feelings from getting bottled-up. In the presence of a dying person, or a distressed or bereaved relative, you will rarely feel totally at ease. There are times, of course, when spontaneous behaviour does occur, when emotions are shared directly with clients or relatives, but these are not normally everyday events. More often you will be working under considerable strain because you can't easily release these emotions. A staff group can provide some opportunities for these tensions to be dealt with.

Helpful, supportive attitudes

Whether within a support group or not, colleagues and managers should try to display constructive attitudes. This means that staff who are feeling distressed about the death of a client should be allowed to express these feelings. They should not be made to feel guilty or inadequate. Care workers and clients share similar concerns about death and it would be surprising if staff were to be unaffected. If proper support is not offered, the danger is that staff may withdraw from involvement with clients who are dying. 'To get close to someone is to risk feeling pain later – so don't get close in the first place' sums up this attitude. With support, however, care workers can learn to cope with the strong emotions surrounding death. Rather than trying to avoid the unavoidable pain of grief and bereavement it is better to accept them as a necessary part of life. In this way you, together with clients and relatives, can grow and learn from the experience.

ACTIVITY

If you have had no experience of dealing with clients who are dying, or of dealing with bereaved relatives, discuss the care issues with your supervisor and experienced colleagues. Find out their views on the following:

- When talking about death with relatives, what language should you use – 'passed on', 'died' or what? Should you use the term that you prefer, or follow whatever the relatives use?

- What do you say if a client asks you whether he or she is dying?
- Should you raise the subject of death or wait for the client to do this first?

These are difficult questions, with no easy answers, so don't worry if you seem not to be able to find quick solutions – no one else has either.

5 Quality care

Quality care: *Good practice and how to maintain it*

During recent years there has been a growing interest in how to make sure that clients receive the best quality care available. The more vulnerable the clients, the more important this is. For instance, confused older people will not be able to complain for themselves and must depend on the advocacy of others.

But how do care providers know how well they are doing? As section 3.6 shows, local authorities have responsibilities to inspect care homes regularly. Reports are written after each inspection and managers can benefit from them. Although this is one way of trying to improve standards, it's not enough on its own. What other methods are there for measuring and improving quality?

Taking personal responsibility

The relationship between client and care worker is at the heart of quality of care. This is also the aspect most obvious to the client. Clients cannot always judge whether care is technically correct but they normally know whether they are being treated with kindness and respect. Be aware of your own standards of performance and ensure that they do not fall below an acceptable level. What, however, is an 'acceptable level'?

One way of starting to answer this question is for all staff to discuss the quality of care they are providing and to agree specific standards.

Setting standards

A standard is a statement of what you want to achieve. Standards can be set about any aspect of care. The first task is to choose an area of care to work on – one where you think improvement is needed and possible.

These are some of the questions that need to be asked before agreeing standards:

- What resources do we need to provide good-quality care?
- What systems of care should we put into practice?
- What results do we expect to achieve?
- How can we measure our achievements?

Here are some examples of standards:

- Each client will be assessed within 24 hours of being admitted. A care plan will be prepared within 48 hours.
- Clients from different ethnic groups will be encouraged to carry out their particular religious practices.

- Meals will be served in such a way as to allow clients to enjoy their meals at their own pace.
- Clients will be encouraged to choose their own general practitioner and dentist.
- Daily newspapers will be available in languages to meet the needs of all clients.

Standards should be achievable. You may wish to improve care in particular ways, but these must be possible in practice. Time is precious and there is no point wasting it on setting unrealistic standards.

Implementing standards

However, agreeing standards is just the start. How will these standards be implemented and how will they be measured? How well are we doing on these measures at the moment? These questions imply choosing ways of measuring standards. This ought to be done at the time that the standard is written. Here are a few suggestions for measuring success.

Your main customers are the clients and their relatives. Others might be staff, either those within the care setting or care professionals who visit occasionally, such as doctors or community nurses. How can you get the views of the customers?

- Ask clients both formally and informally. It is good practice to ask clients how they think things are going. This can be part of everyday conversation, or more systematic methods can be used. Questionnaires are one way of achieving structured feedback. They should be short and simple, and can be handed or sent to clients, relatives and other visitors.
- A suggestion book will allow the customers to note their ideas for improvements.
- When clients are able and willing, they should be encouraged to form a residents' or clients' group. This might serve several purposes, but one should certainly be to provide a view on the quality of care they are receiving.
- Outside people can be asked to visit regularly to assess care. It is a way of getting a fresh view of events and conditions, in addition to the official inspections carried out by local authorities.

Searching for good practice is hard work because expectations are rising all the time in response to new thinking about care. Nevertheless, it is precisely in this search that the rewards of caring are also to be found.

ACTIVITY

Try your hand at writing standards. You will first need to choose an area of care, for example 'assessment', 'meal-times' or 'meeting spiritual needs'. The standards should be:

- achievable;

- measurable (ask yourself how);
- simple to understand.

Setting standards is about agreeing what needs to be done – so arrange to do this exercise with colleagues.

This is a questionnaire used by a small care home, designed to be sent to relatives and visiting professional care staff.

● ● ●   HOW ARE WE DOING?   ● ● ●

Every so often, it is important for us to find out how well we are doing. One of the best ways is to ask you, as a visitor to Daneleigh House, what you feel about the level of care we provide.

Please feel quite free to write whatever you wish. If you don't want to add your name that's fine too. We have enclosed a stamped, addressed envelope for your reply.

1   What do you feel about the general atmosphere in the house? For example, are you made to feel welcome? Do residents seem involved and active?

1   ....
....

2   Are you satisfied with the level of care that your relative has received? Could you give any examples?

2   ....
....

3   Would you like to see improvements in any aspect of our care? If so, please could you say what these are?

3   ....
....

4   What is the best thing about Daneleigh House?

4   ....
....

5   What is the worst thing about Daneleigh House?

5   ....
....

6   Please feel free to add any other comments here:

6   ....
....

Name: ....
(leave blank if you prefer)

Thank you for your help. It is much appreciated. Any other comments you would like to make, at any time, will always be welcomed.

Reading on . . .

★ Section 3.2 stresses the importance of beliefs and values in providing a good standard of care. The Social Services Inspectorate has produced a number of reports on standards and quality. Information can be obtained from HMSO, PO Box 276, London SW8 5DT (071–873 0011).

★ Another organisation actively involved in promoting quality of care is the King's Fund Centre, 126 Albert Street, London NW1 7NF. Although their work is concerned with health care, many of their publications are easily applied to care in general.

ACTIVITY

Read through the questionnaire given here. How successful do you think it might be? Can you suggest improvements? Design a questionnaire for use in your own care setting.

Appendix 1: How to find out more

There are a great many organisations concerned, directly or indirectly, with the care and welfare of older people. Only a relatively small number can be mentioned here. Most have already been mentioned in the text. All organisations would very much appreciate a stamped, addressed envelope so that they can send information to you.

Age Concern
Astral House
1268 London Road
London SW16 4EJ

Tel. 081–679 8000
Fax. 081–679 6069

Centre for Policy on Ageing
25–31 Ironmonger Row
London EC1V 3QP

Tel. 071–253 1787
Fax. 071–490 4206

Commission for Racial Equality
Elliot House
10–12 Allington Street
London SW1E 5EH

Tel. 071–828 7022

Counsel and Care for the Elderly
Twyman House
16 Bonny Street
London NW1 9PG

Tel. 071–485 1550

Disabled Living Foundation
380–384 Harrow Road
London W9 2HU

Tel. 071–289 6111
Fax. 071–266 2922

Help the Aged
St James's Walk
London EC1R OBE

Tel. 071–253 0253

Homecraft Supplies Limited
Low Moor Estate
Kirkby-in-Ashfield
Nottinghamshire NG17 7JZ

Tel. 0623 757955

National Extension College
18 Brooklands Avenue
Cambridge CB2 2HN

Tel. 0223 316644
Fax. 0223 313586

Nottingham Rehab
Ludlow Hill Road
West Bridgford
Nottingham NG2 6HD

Tel. 0602 452345
Fax. 0602 452124

Open University
Walton Hall
Milton Keynes
MK7 6AA

Tel. 0908 653231

University of the Third Age
1 Stockwell Green
London SW9 9JF

Tel. 071–737 2541

Winslow Press
Telford Road
Bicester
Oxfordshire OX6 0TS

Tel. 0869 244644
Fax. 0869 320040

Appendix 2: NVQs/SVQs

The Care Sector Consortium has developed 'occupational standards' for workers in the care sector. These describe the outcomes that workers need to achieve to become competent. Selected standards have been grouped together to form qualifications – NVQs or SVQs – at different levels. So far, qualifications have been produced at levels 2 and 3.

At each level there is a set of core units which all candidates have to be assessed on and a choice of other units (known as endorsements) which cover the competences needed by workers in particular care roles, such as 'supporting independence', 'rehabilitative care' or 'terminal care'. For each competence, 'underpinning knowledge' is needed – for example, to be safe in helping incontinent clients, you should understand the causes of incontinence.

This workbook provides underpinning knowledge for all of the core units at levels 2 and 3, and much of that needed for a number of the endorsements likely to be taken by workers caring for older clients.

The core units are listed here with examples of the sections in the book where you will find references to them.

Level 2 core units	Sections of this book
O Promote equality for all individuals	2.3, 3.9, 3.15, 4.2, 4.3, 4.4, 4.9, 4.28
Z1 Contribute to the protection of individuals from abuse	3.7, 4.5, 4.9, 4.25, 4.26, 4.27
W2 Contribute to the ongoing support of clients and others significant to them	4.6, 4.7, 4.10, 4.11
W3 Support clients in transition due to their care requirements	3.3, 3.4, 3.5, 3.6, 3.8, 3.16, 3.17, 3.18
U4 Contribute to the health, safety and security of individuals and their environment	3.4, 3.15, 3.16, 3.17, 4.15 to 4.27
U5 Obtain, transmit and store information relating to the delivery of a care service	3.9, 3.10, 3.14, 3.15

Level 3 core units	*Sections of this book*
O Promote equality for all individuals	2.3, 3.9, 3.15, 4.2, 4.3, 4.4, 4.9, 4.28
Z1 Contribute to the protection of individuals from abuse	3.7, 4.5, 4.9, 4.25, 4.26, 4.27
Z3 Contribute to the management of aggressive and abusive behaviour	4.5, 4.26, 4.27
Z4 Promote communication with clients where there are communication difficulties	3.15, 4.1, 4.2, 4.3, 4.4
Z8 Support clients when they are distressed	4.1, 4.4, 4.5, 4.23, 4.24, 4.25, 4.29, 4.30, 4.31
Y2 Enable clients to make use of available services and information	3.13, 3.16, 3.17, 3.18, 4.7
V1 Contribute to the planning and monitoring of service delivery	3.3, 3.9, 3.10, 3.11, 3.12, 3.13, 3.14, 3.15
U4 Contribute to the health, safety and security of individuals and their environment	3.4, 3.15, 3.16, 3.17, 4.15 to 4.27
U5 Obtain, transmit and store information relating to the delivery of a care service	3.9, 3.10, 3.14, 3.15

Bibliography

Most of these publications have been cited already in the text – but it will be helpful to be able to refer to them quickly here. A few other books are also included, so that you can broaden your reading on this subject.

Aggleton, Peter and Helen Chalmers 1986. *Nursing Models and the Nursing Process*. London: Macmillan Education.

Bristow, Phillip 1989. *Famous Ways to Grow Old*. Mitcham: Age Concern.

Care Sector Consortium 1991. *Integration Project – Draft Occupational Standards*. Produced for the Care Sector Consortium by Prime Research & Development Ltd and VTDS.

Centre for Policy on Ageing 1984. *Home Life: a code of practice for residential care*. London: Centre for Policy on Ageing.

Chapman, Christine 1985. *Theory of Nursing: practical application*. London: Harper & Row.

Department of Health Social Services Inspectorate 1990. *Caring for Quality: guidance on standards for residential homes for elderly people*. London: Her Majesty's Stationery Office.

Erikson, Erik 1963. *Childhood and Society*. Harmondsworth: Penguin.

Family Policy Studies Centre 1991. *An Ageing Population*, Fact Sheet 2 (September 1991). Help the Aged.

Fennell, Graham, Chris Phillipson and Helen Evers 1988. *The Sociology of Old Age*. Milton Keynes: Open University Press.

Forrest, Darle 1989. The experience of caring. In *Journal of Advanced Nursing* 14, 815–823.

Harris, Diana 1990. *Sociology of Aging*. New York: Harper & Row.

Harvey, Marilyn 1990. *Who's Confused?* Birmingham: PEPAR Publications.

HMSO 1989. *Caring for People*, Cmnd 849. London: Her Majesty's Stationery Office.

Hooker, Susan 1990. *Caring for Elderly People*. London: Routledge.

Johnston, Susanna and Chris Phillipson (eds) 1983. *Older Learners*. London: Bedford Square Press (for Help the Aged Education Department).

Mace, Nancy and Peter Rabins 1985. *The 36-Hour Day*. London: Edward Arnold with Age Concern.

Maslow, Abraham 1970. *Motivation and Personality*. New York: Harper & Row.

Midwinter, Eric 1982. *Age is Opportunity: education and older people*. London: Centre for Policy on Ageing.

Neill, June 1989. *Assessing Elderly People for Residential Care: a practical guide*. London: National Institute for Social Work.

Nelson-Jones, Richard 1986. *Human Relationship Skills*. London: Holt, Rinehart & Winston.

Norman, Alison 1985. *Triple Jeopardy: growing old in a second homeland*. London: Centre for Policy on Ageing.

Nussbaum, Jon F., Teresa Thompson and James D. Robinson 1989. *Communication and Aging*. New York: Harper & Row.

Nutrition Advisory Service for the Elderly 1988. *Eating a Way into the 90s*. British Dietetic Association.

Pearson, Alan and Barbara Vaughan 1986. *Nursing Models for Practice*. London: Heinemann.

Puner, M. 1974. *To the Good Long Life: what we know about growing old*. London: Macmillan. [Quoted in Fennell *et al.* 1988.]

Rimmer, Lorna 1982. *Reality Orientation: principles and practice*. Bicester: Winslow Press.

Schaie, K. Warner and Sherry L. Willis 1991. *Adult Development and Aging*. New York: Harper Collins.

Seabrook, Jeremy 1980. *The Way We Are*. Mitcham: Age Concern.

Squires, Amanda (ed.) 1991. *Multicultural Health Care and Rehabilitation of Older People*. London: Edward Arnold with Age Concern.

Wynne-Harley, Deirdre 1991. *Living Dangerously*. London: Centre for Policy on Ageing.

Zwanenberg, Fiona von 1988. *Take Care of Yourself*. London and Bicester: Winslow Press and Help the Aged.

Index